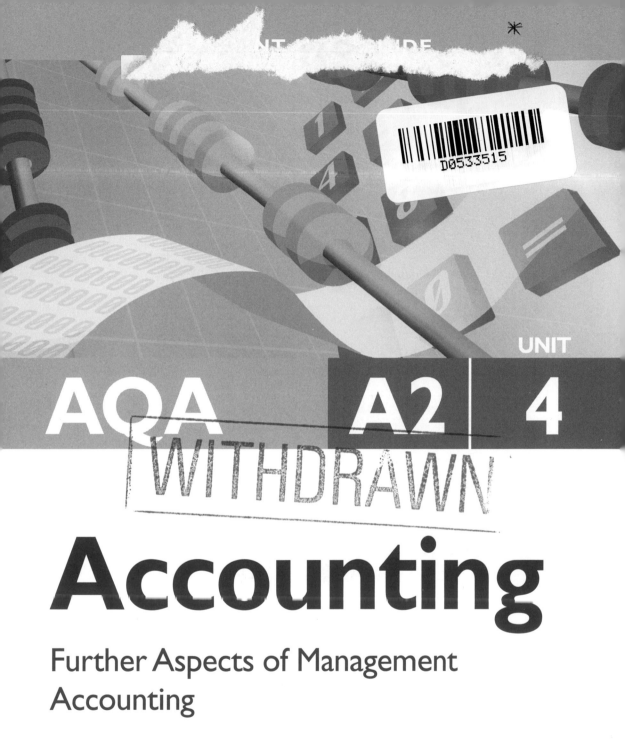

AQA A2 UNIT 4

WITHDRAWN

Accounting

Further Aspects of Management
Accounting

Ian Harrison

Philip Allan Updates, an imprint of Hodder Education, an Hachette UK company, Market Place, Deddington, Oxfordshire OX15 0SE

Orders

Bookpoint Ltd, 130 Milton Park, Abingdon, Oxfordshire OX14 4SB
tel: 01235 827720
fax: 01235 400454
e-mail: uk.orders@bookpoint.co.uk

Lines are open 9.00 a.m.–5.00 p.m., Monday to Saturday, with a 24-hour message answering service. You can also order through the Philip Allan Updates website: www.philipallan.co.uk

© Philip Allan Updates 2010

ISBN 978-0-340-95821-6

First printed 2010

Impression number 5 4 3 2 1

Year 2014 2013 2012 2011 2010

This guide has been written specifically to support students preparing for the AQA A2 Accounting Unit 4 examination. The content has been neither approved nor endorsed by AQA and remains the sole responsibility of the author.

Typeset by DC Graphic Design Ltd, Swanley Village, Kent.

Printed by MPG Books, Bodmin

Hachette UK's policy is to use papers that are natural, renewable and recyclable products and made from wood grown in sustainable forests. The logging and manufacturing processes are expected to conform to the environmental regulations of the country of origin.

P01616

Contents

Introduction

■ ■ ■

Content Guidance

■ ■ ■

Questions and Answers

Introduction

About this guide

This student guide is an ideal resource for your revision of AQA Accounting A2 Unit 4: Further Aspects of Management Accounting.

The guide is in three sections:
- This **Introduction** covers the aims and assessment of the A2 course and outlines study strategies and revision techniques
- **Content Guidance** covers the content of Unit 4.
- **Questions and Answers** provides ten questions; each question focuses on a specific area of content. Each question is based on the format of the A2 examination papers and is followed by two sample answers (an A-grade and a lower-grade response) together with comments by the examiner.

You should read the relevant topic area in the Content Guidance section before you attempt a question from the Questions and Answers section. Only read the specimen answers after you have attempted the question yourself.

Aims of the A2 qualification

The A2 accounting course aims to encourage you to develop:
- an understanding of the importance of effective accounting information systems and an awareness of their limitations
- a critical approach to the appraisal of financial issues and business practices
- an understanding of the purposes, principles, concepts and techniques of accounting
- the transferable skills of numeracy, communication, ICT, application, presentation, interpretation, analysis and evaluation in an accounting context
- an appreciation of the effects of economic, legal, ethical, social, environmental and technological influences on accounting decisions
- a capacity for methodical and critical thought, which serves as an end in itself, as well as a basis for further study of accounting and other subjects

Assessment

Remember that the course is designed to allow you to show your ability and to use your skills. All the accounting examination papers test the following assessment objectives in the context of the specification content to varying degrees:
- **knowledge and understanding** of the accounting principles, concepts and techniques within familiar and unfamiliar situations

- **application** of knowledge and understanding — of all the accounting content that is covered in the course — to familiar and unfamiliar situations
- **analysis and evaluation** by ordering, interpreting and analysing information using appropriate formats, taking into account the possible effect of all factors, internal and external, to the business — making judgements, decisions and recommendations based on the assessment of alternative courses of action that might be influenced by internal and external factors

Quality of written communication (QWC)

On each paper, 4 marks are awarded for the quality of written communication. The marks are split equally between written communication (for prose answers) and quality of presentation (for numerical answers). These marks are awarded in specific questions that are clearly identified on the examination paper.

The specification requires that you use:
- text that is legible, and that your spelling, punctuation and grammar ensure that the meaning is clear
- a form and style of writing that is appropriate to the purpose and to the complexity of the subject matter
- information in a clear, coherent way and that specialist vocabulary is used where appropriate

Unit 4

Unit 4 contributes 25% of the marks for the A-level qualification. It is a 2-hour written paper and there are 90 raw marks available. There will be four compulsory questions. Each question will have a variable number of sub-questions and will carry a variable number of marks.

The approximate weightings for Unit 4 are:

Knowledge and understanding	20%	17 marks
Application	50%	43 marks
Analysis and evaluation	30%	26 marks
	100%	86 marks (plus 4 marks for QWC)

Compared with AS Unit 1, fewer marks are available for knowledge and understanding and hence more emphasis is required on analysis and evaluation.

You can learn to recognise the marks allocated to the higher order skills of analysis and evaluation by the use of certain 'trigger words'. The most common trigger words are:
- **Advise** — suggest solutions to a problem and justify your solution.
- **Analyse** — identify the characteristics of the information given.
- **Assess** — make an informed judgement based on information supplied in the question.

- **Discuss** — present advantages and disadvantages or strengths and weaknesses of a particular course of action and arrive at a conclusion based on the question scenario.
- **To what extent** — similar to 'discuss' but requiring a judgement based on the likelihood of potential outcomes and effects on the given scenario.

It is important that answers requiring analysis and evaluation result in a judgement being made. You use these skills almost every day. For example, you might say to a friend, 'I think we should go bowling tonight because...' — that is a judgement. You might add to that an analysis of the reasons why you think you should go bowling: '... because the lads we met there last time said that they would be there tonight too and we had such a good time with them last week'.

Content Guidance

The Content Guidance section of this guide outlines the topic areas covered in Unit 4. This unit builds on the assessment objectives covered in the AS course but the assessment objectives will now be applied to more complex situations and content. (See 'Synoptic assessment' below.)

Synoptic assessment

Synoptic assessment tests your ability to see relationships between different topic areas included in the subject content. It will be tested by using decision-making or problem-solving situations where you will be required to draw together knowledge and understanding of content areas learned in different parts of your A-level accounting course. In Unit 4 you could be tested on issues relating to AS Unit 2. The focus of the synoptic questions in this unit will emanate from the topics in Unit 4, although questions may draw on related topics covered in Unit 2. However, candidates are always rewarded for employing, in their answers, relevant knowledge, understanding and skills learned in any of the other units.

Stretch and challenge

There is a requirement at A2 that you should be stretched to reach your full potential and be presented with questions that present a challenging situation. This will be achieved in questions that require evaluation and the application of knowledge and skills to complex situations.

Revision techniques

Studying and revising for any examination should not be left until the last minute. In order to pass the examination you should make careful notes throughout your course. In accounting, it is important that you practise questions based on each topic area on a regular basis. For example, you must learn the layout of, and be able to produce, a manufacturing account. Furthermore, each topic that you revise should be analysed critically so that making decisions based on information given becomes second nature to you. This is essential as it is where the higher order skill marks can be gained. The examiner will expect an analytical and evaluative approach in your answers where appropriate.

Revision is a continuous process. Revise topics on a regular basis rather than waiting until the last few weeks before the examination. Your teacher will have helped you throughout your course by setting homework and by giving regular tests in class time. Use both types of work to ensure that you really do understand that particular topic. Revise the topic to be covered in the test or homework before you attempt it. When your work is returned, note carefully your teacher's comments and try to put right any basic errors that have been highlighted. If there are issues that you do not understand, ask your teacher to explain while the problem is still fresh in your mind.

Use each piece of work to build up a bank of knowledge and skills that you may be able to apply to subsequent pieces of work. As a subject, accounting is rather like a detective solving a crime; the pieces of information collected some weeks ago might help to solve today's problem. Also bear in mind that there is a limited number of accounting problems that you can be asked to solve; the names and numbers will be different in each question but the method that you use should be familiar to you.

There is no best way of revising. All students are different and you must find the methods that suit you best. However, you must *learn* the key concepts for each topic. This is usually easier that you might first think; the difficult part is applying the knowledge to the questions set by the examiner.

Draw up a revision programme well before your examination. Draw up a weekly plan that identifies a number of instances when you can devote at least an hour of uninterrupted time to your revision (switch off your mobile phone). Remember that, for most students, accounting will not be the only subject for revision — take this into account when making your plans.

Try to find the times of day that best suit you. If you are at school or college, try to use your free time during the day for revision — this will free up time in the evening when you may wish to see friends. Build this into your plans. In school or college, find a quiet place in the library or in an empty classroom. You may not like working in a quiet atmosphere but it will be quiet in the examination hall and therefore you should get used to working in those conditions.

Once you have drawn up your programme, try to stick to it. A regular routine works best and pays the greatest dividends. If you lose concentration while revising, take a break. Alternatively, revise a different topic or subject for a while.

Varying your method of revision should help you to concentrate for longer periods of time. Try using some of the following:
- Read aloud.

- Explain topics to yourself.
- Test yourself.
- Use a friend and test each other.
- Use a friend to bounce ideas or answers off (take care that this technique does not end up in a gossip session).
- Summarise answers to written questions.
- Practise parts of questions that build up to a whole question.
- Practise questions under quiet exam conditions, i.e. time-restricted.

Ask yourself the question: 'Could I explain this topic to someone who does not know anything about accounting?' If you can honestly answer 'yes', you probably understand the topic and only need to read it through several times during revision. If your answer is 'no', you need to spend more time thoroughly revising the topic.

Use the following tips as a basis for your revision programme:
- Revise only one topic at each session.
- When you get nearer to the examination date, try to extend the amount of time spent revising; you may have back-to-back examinations in one session and therefore need to practise holding your concentration for long periods of time.
- Read this guide and use your textbook plus your class notes to build up a comprehensive body of knowledge on each topic area. Summarise the key points.
- Attempt the questions provided in the Questions and Answers section of this guide. Check your answers against the example answers provided. Read the examiner comments to find out how the candidates could have improved their answers.
- Remember that, like an athlete training for the Olympic Games, you have been training for these examinations for some time. Don't miss out on a good result through lack of training (revision).

Content
Guidance

This section of the guide outlines the topic areas of Unit 4. They are:

- manufacturing accounts
  - provision for unrealised profit
- marginal, absorption and activity based costing
  - the terms used in cost and management accounting
  - absorption costing
  - marginal costing
  - calculation of break-even
  - activity based costing (ABC)
- standard costing
- capital investment appraisal
- budgets and budgetary control
- social accounting

Manufacturing accounts

By this stage of your studies of accounting you will have produced many income statements. Income statements are prepared for businesses that trade, i.e. they purchase goods and resell them.

Businesses that make goods and sell them need more information than is shown in the income statements that you are used to producing. The 'extra' information is shown in a manufacturing account that appears before the income statement. A manufacturing account shows the costs associated with the production process. It shows the costs of running and maintaining the factory in which the product is made. A manufacturing account is the link between cost accounting and financial accounting. It has its place in both branches of accounting.

A manufacturing account itemises all of the factory costs associated with the production process. It has two main sections.

The prime cost section

This section contains all the costs that can be directly attributed to the product. These are known as direct costs (or variable costs) and include:
- the cost of raw materials
- the wages of production workers
- other direct expenses, for example manufacturing royalties

The overheads section

This section contains the payments made for all the other activities that are necessary to run the factory. These are not of a general nature and are essential in running the factory. However, they cannot be directly attributed to the product being made. These overheads could include any expenses incurred because of the factory's existence, for example:
- factory rent and business rates
- supervisors' wages
- depreciation of any plant and machinery used in the factory

Overheads that do not contribute to the running of the factory are entered in the income statement. Examples of these would include:
- selling and distribution costs
- wages of office personnel
- depreciation of IT equipment

It is important that you can classify items of expenditure into those occurring in the factory and those incurred by the office. You then need to be able to segregate factory expenditure into:

- prime costs
- overheads (other factory costs)

If you can do this quickly and efficiently, you can produce a manufacturing account.

The most common error that students make is to deduct the overheads from prime cost. Do not be one of those students. Remember that the manufacturing account is a list of *all* expenses incurred in running a factory.

This total is called total production cost.

Inventories in a manufacturing business

There are usually three types of inventory:

(1) Raw materials — these are the 'ingredients' that have yet to enter the production process.
(2) Work-in-progress — products that are partly finished and still need further processing before they reach their finished form.
(3) Finished goods — these are goods that are waiting to be sold.

The three different types of inventory appear in different sections of the financial statements.

Since raw materials are used in the factory and partly finished goods have not yet completed their journey through the factory, both appear in the manufacturing account. The opening and closing inventories of raw materials are incorporated in the prime cost section. The inventory of work-in-progress comprises adjustments that are shown after the total factory overheads have been added to prime cost.

The inventory of finished goods appears in the income statement since these are the goods that the business trades with.

Provision for unrealised profit

Some manufacturing businesses transfer the goods that they produce to the warehouse ready for selling to customers at a price that is greater than the total production cost. The difference between the transfer price and the total cost of producing the goods is a profit on manufacturing (or a profit earned by the factory).

This profit loading gives credit to the factory personnel for their part in contributing to the overall profitability of the business (it is an attempt to recognise the part that the factory has played as one section of the business).

Total gross profit of a business stems from:

- manufacturing efficiently
- selling goods at a price that is higher than production costs

The profit loading can be:

- a percentage of the total production cost or
- the price to be paid if the goods had been purchased from another manufacturing business

Example 1 Percentage of total production cost:

John manufactures a component for the motor industry. Finished goods are transferred to the income statement at cost plus 20%. He provides the following information for the year ended 31 January 2010.

	£000
Sales	4 760
Inventory of finished goods at 1 February 2009	32
Inventory of finished goods at 31 January 2010	40
Total production cost	2 100

Prepare extracts from:

(a) the manufacturing account for the year ended 31 January 2010

(b) the income statement to show how the transfer is dealt with

Answer:

(a)　　*John: Extract from the manufacturing account for the year ended 31 January 2010*

	£
Total production cost	2 100 000
Manufacturing profit	420 000
Transfer price	2 520 000

(b)　　*John: Extract from the income statement for the year ended 31 January 2010*

	£	£
Sales		4 760 000
Less cost of sales		
Inventory of finished goods at 1 February 2009	32 000	
Transfer price of manufactured goods	2 520 000	
	2 552 000	
Inventory of finished goods at 31 January 2010	40 000	2 512 000
Gross profit on trading		2 248 000

Example 2 Price to be paid if the goods were purchased from another manufacturing business:

Jayne provides the following information for her manufacturing business for the year ended 28 February 2010.

She transfers goods from her factory to the income statement at a price dictated by the market for her goods if she were to purchase them rather than manufacture them.

	£000
Sales	7 630
Inventory of finished goods at 1 March 2009	87
Inventory of finished goods at 28 February 2010	96
Total production cost	3 780
Market price of goods if purchased from an 'outside' supplier	4 370

Prepare extracts from:

(a) the manufacturing account for the year ended 28 February 2010

(b) the income statement showing the gross profit on trading

Answer:

(a)   *Jayne: Extract from the manufacturing account for the year ended 28 February 2010*

	£000
Total production costs	3 780
Manufacturing profit	590
Transfer price	4 370

(b)   *Jayne: Extract from the income statement for the year ended 28 February 2010*

	£000	£000
Sales		7 630
Less cost of sales		
Inventory of finished goods at 1 March 2009	87	
Transfer price of manufactured goods	4 370	
	4 457	
Inventory of finished goods at 28 February 2010	96	4 361
Gross profit on trading		3 269

Inventories that are passed for sale must be valued in order to prepare the cost of sales section of the income statement. The sales staff may value the inventory of finished goods at the cost to them, i.e. the transfer price from the factory. This 'cost', as we have seen, is designed to give credit to the factory personnel for contributing to the overall profit of the business.

If the inventory of finished goods is valued at the transfer price, any valuation will include the profit loading.

Valuing inventory of finished goods at cost plus a profit loading contravenes two accounting concepts:
- The concept of prudence — in Unit 3 we saw that inventories should be valued at the lower of cost and net realisable value.

- The realisation concept states that profit cannot be recognised until the title to goods passes to a customer (it is as yet unrealised).

If the valuation of inventories of finished goods contains an element of factory profit, it must be deleted in the income statement, otherwise profits will be overstated by the amount of the unrealised profit.

The inventory shown as a current asset will also be overstated so the inventory of finished goods shown in the balance sheet must also be shown net of the unrealised profit.

The provision account in itself is similar in appearance to all other provision accounts that you have prepared during your studies of accounting.

Example:

Helen Khoo manufactures plastic boxes for the electronics industry. She provides the following information for the year ended 31 December 2009.

	£
Sales to electronic industry	1 762 500
Transfer price from manufacturing account	1 066 000
Selling and distribution and administration costs	477 430

Additional information:

Inventories	31 December 2008 £	31 December 2009 £
Raw materials	9 760	10 120
Work-in-progress	8 270	8 530
Finished goods	22 100	25 350

Helen transfers her goods from the manufacturing account to the income statement at cost plus 30%.

Prepare:

(a) a provision for unrealised profit account for the year ended 31 December 2009

(b) an income statement for the year ended 31 December 2009

(c) a balance sheet extract at 31 December 2009 showing the treatment of inventories

Answer:

(a)   *Provision for unrealised profit*

		1 Jan 2009 Balance b/d	5 100 w1
31 Dec 2009 Balance c/d	5 850 w2	31 Dec 2009 Inc stat	750
	5 850		5 850
		1 Jan 2010 balance b/d	5 850

w1 $22\ 100 \times \dfrac{30}{130} = 5100$ w2 $25\ 350 \times \dfrac{30}{130} = 5850$

(b) **Income statement for Helen Khoo for the year ended 31 December 2009**

	£	£
Sales		1 762 500
Less cost of sales		
Inventory 1 January 2009	22 100	
Transfer from manufacturing account	1 066 000	
	1 088 100	
Inventory 31 December 2009	25 350	1 062 750
Gross profit on trading		699 750
Gross profit on manufacturing	246 000 w3	
Less provision for unrealised profit	750	245 250
Total gross profit		945 000
Less expenses		477 430
Profit for year		467 570

w3 $1\,066\,000 \times \dfrac{30}{130} = 246\,000$

(c)   **Balance sheet extract at 31 December 2009**

	£	£
Current assets		
Inventories		
Raw materials		10 120
Work-in-progress		8 530
Finished goods	25 350	
Less provision for unrealised profit	5 850	19 500
		38 150

Marginal, absorption and activity based costing

Terms

It is important that you learn the terms used in cost accounting. You may find this difficult initially, but stick with it. Practise definitions regularly and you will find that it is not as difficult as you first think. If you have a spare moment waiting for transport, go over the definition in your head. Flash cards are useful here. Remember that a definition is an explanation of the term; it is not an example. Having said that, if you find it difficult to express your thoughts precisely, an example may be used to support your thoughts. For example, the following is not a definition:

'Fixed costs are rent.'

However, the following would indicate to the examiner that you understand the concept of fixed costs by virtue of giving a reasonable example:

'Fixed costs don't change very often, for example rent doesn't change if you increase production or decrease production but the landlord could put it up sometime in the future.'

Even if a question does not ask for a definition, you may find it useful to include one as it can help you to clarify your thoughts and get you started on answering the question.

The hard part is applying the terms to the problems that appear in questions set by the examiner.

Direct costs can be directly identified or associated with a cost unit. They are defined by CIMA as 'expenditure that can be economically identified with a specific saleable cost unit'. Direct labour means workers whose work can be identified with the raw materials that will become the finished product. Direct labour costs are therefore directly attributable to a unit of production and can be easily traced to that finished product. They are part of the prime costs shown in a manufacturing account.

Indirect costs cannot be directly identified or associated with a cost unit. However, their payment is essential in order to run the factory. They appear under the heading of factory overheads in a manufacturing account. Indirect labour costs are the costs incurred in the employment of factory staff whose work cannot be directly identified with the final product. Examples would include the wages of factory cleaners, maintenance engineers, supervisory staff etc. Indirect material costs are the costs of materials that cannot be directly identified with the finished product, for example cleaning materials, machine lubricants etc. Also included as indirect costs under the heading of factory overheads would be factory rent and rates, factory insurance, depreciation of factory plant and machinery; in fact, all costs incurred in running a factory that cannot be classified as direct costs.

Semi-variable costs are those costs that contain an element that remains fixed despite changes in levels of business activity and an element that will change in direct relation to changes in levels of business activity. These costs appear as factory overheads in a manufacturing account.

Fixed costs remain the same despite changes in the level of business activity. They are sometimes referred to as period costs since they are time-based. In the short run, fixed costs tend not to change. (They *may* change. For example, a new warehouse or production line may have to be brought into play if a business expands causing rents, power charges etc. to increase.) In the long run, fixed costs often change when landlords increase rent and business rates increase.

Marginal costs are the costs of producing one extra unit. For example:

Costs for 10 000 units

	£
Raw materials	15 000
Direct labour	40 000
Royalties	1 000
	56 000

Marginal cost per unit = £5.60

The bulk of marginal costs tends to be also variable costs but could include extra fixed costs and extra semi-variable costs.

Contribution is the difference between selling price and variable costs. It is used firstly to cover fixed costs; anything remaining after fixed costs have been covered is profit. It can be calculated in total in a marginal cost statement or per unit. This is used as a management tool in marginal costing.

Break-even is the level of sales revenue and/or the number of units sold in which the business expenses are covered by revenue — that is, where the business makes neither a profit nor loss on the particular product.

Absorption costing

It is important that a manufacturing business is able to cover all its costs and charge a price for the product(s) that enables it to be profitable and so ensure its continued existence.

You should be able to define and explain the following terms.

Absorption costing is a system of absorbing both direct costs and overheads into the total production cost of each saleable unit produced in a factory.

Cost centre. CIMA defines a cost centre as 'a production or service location, function or activity or item of equipment whose costs may be attributed to cost units'. So a cost centre may be a department, a machine or a person working in the business.

A **cost unit** is a product that absorbs the cost centre's overhead costs. A cost centre might be the department producing packets of chocolate biscuits, while the cost unit would be a packet of the chocolate biscuits produced.

Allocation of overheads is the process of charging whole items of expenditure to a cost centre or a cost unit. The costs are easily identified as deriving from the cost centre or cost unit.

Apportionment of overheads is the process by which some overhead costs that cannot be allocated are charged to cost centres or cost units using some rational basis.

Example:

The directors of the Kunal Manufacturing Company Ltd provide the following budgeted information for April for the two departments operated by the company.

	£
Raw materials	750 000
Rent and rates	72 000
Power	210 000
Direct wages	800 000
Supervisory wages	160 000
Depreciation of factory machinery	120 000

Additional information:

	Department A	Department B
Total factory area	30 000 m²	150 000 m²
Power used	35 000 kWh	70 000 kWh
Cost of machinery	£400 000	£800 000
Staff employed	32	8

Prepare an overhead analysis sheet for April.

Answer:

Overhead	Total cost £	Basis of apportionment	Dept A £	Dept B £
Rent and rates	72 000	Floor area	12 000	60 000
Power	210 000	kWh	70 000	140 000
Supervisory wages	160 000	Number of staff	128 000	32 000
Depreciation	120 000	Cost of machinery	40 000	80 000
	562 000		250 000	312 000

Note: raw materials and direct wages do not appear in the overhead analysis sheet since they are direct costs and can therefore be allocated. Only the overheads that need to be apportioned between the cost centres are included.

Transfer of service department costs

Service cost centres provide services that support production departments — for example, maintenance, canteen facilities and personnel departments. They are not directly involved in the production process and so cannot incorporate their costs into a selling price for their product. However, their costs must be recovered by the business.

Service department costs are recovered by apportioning to each production department part of the total cost of running the service department. The bases used depend on the service provided. The process means that each production department will recover its own overheads and a portion of the service departments' overheads.

Example:

The following information relates to the three departments of Ashish and Sneh Ltd.

	Production departments		Canteen
	A	B	
Number of employees	100	190	10
Floor area	10 000 m²	15 000 m²	5000 m²
Cost of machinery	£120 000	£360 000	£40 000
Power used in each department	40 000 kWh	80 000 kWh	10 000 kWh

The direct costs involved in running the canteen are expected to be £50 000.

The factory overheads for the three departments for the year ended 31 July 2010 are expected to be:

	£
Rent	12 000
Heat and light	60 000
Supervisory wages	900 000
Power	390 000
Depreciation	104 000

Prepare an overhead analysis sheet showing the apportionment of overheads for the year ended 31 July 2010.

Answer:

Overhead	Cost	Basis of	Dept A	Dept B	Canteen
	£	apportionment	£	£	£
Direct costs	50 000	Allocation			50 000
Rent	12 000	Floor area	4 000	6 000	2 000
Heat and light	60 000	Floor area	20 000	30 000	10 000
Supervisory wages	900 000	Number of staff	300 000	570 000	30 000
Power	390 000	kWh	120 000	240 000	30 000
Depreciation	104 000	Cost of machinery	24 000	72 000	8 000
	1 516 000		468 000	918 000	130 000
			44 828	85 172	(130 000)
	1 516 000		512 828	1 003 172	–

Note: apportionment takes place because some overheads cannot be directly attributed to a particular cost centre. The direct costs incurred by the canteen need to be recovered because the canteen does not make external sales; these direct costs need to be recovered together with the canteen overheads by apportioning them to the production departments.

Absorption of overheads occurs after overheads have been apportioned to the appropriate cost centres. The amount to be absorbed by each cost unit is known as the overhead absorption rate, or OAR. Although there are a number of methods of calculating the OAR, only two are examined at A-level:

- The **direct labour hour rate** is used when a department (cost centre) is labour intensive — that is, there is little use of machinery, or machine costs are low.
- The **machine hour rate** of absorption is used when production methods are capital intensive or when machine costs are relatively high. It calculates the hours that a machine is used in the production of one unit of output.

Overhead recovery rates are based on predicted business activity and the predicted levels of future overhead costs.

If the prediction of activity and costs are equal to the actual levels of activity and overhead costs, the overheads will be recovered exactly. However, if activity is greater than anticipated and overhead costs are as predicted, or overhead costs are lower than expected while activity is as predicted, there will be an over-recovery of overheads; this is credited to the costing income statement. If the activity is lower than anticipated and overhead costs are as predicted, or overhead costs are higher than expected while activity is as predicted, there will be an under-recovery of overheads; this is debited to the costing income statement.

Other overheads incurred in a business must also be recovered if the manufacturing business is to survive. Selling and distribution costs, administration costs and finance costs are recovered in the mark-up applied to the total cost of goods before they are sold to the final customers.

Example:

The fixed production costs incurred by a manufacturing business are £135 000 per month. The budgeted production for January is expected to be 1200 units.

Each unit of production is expected to take 10 labour hours and 20 minutes of machining to complete.

Calculate the absorption rate using:

(a) the labour hour rate method

(b) the machine hour rate method

Answer:

(a) Labour hour rate method $\dfrac{£135\ 000}{12\ 000}$ = £11.25 per hour

(b) Machine hour rate method $\dfrac{£135\ 000}{400}$ = £337.50 per hour

Marginal costing

Marginal costing makes a clear distinction between fixed costs and variable costs and there is no attempt to apportion any fixed costs to a cost centre or a cost unit. It assumes that fixed costs are time period costs and that the current level of fixed costs has already been covered by other production.

Marginal costs are incurred when one extra unit is produced above the planned level.

Marginal revenues are revenues that are earned by selling one extra unit of production.

Marginal costs are usually made up of the costs of extra materials, extra direct wages and other extra variable costs when production is increased.

Fixed costs will not change when business activity increases.

As you will have observed in your studies, absorption costing allocates and apportions all costs that are expected to occur in running the whole business. These costs are absorbed into the selling price charged to the customer. The key to solving marginal costing problems is the calculation of contribution made by the product(s).

Contribution is the amount by which the selling price exceeds the variable costs incurred. It is not profit but goes toward paying fixed costs; after fixed costs have been covered, any remaining contribution is profit.

Example:

The selling price of a Lert is £10. The following costs are incurred in the production of a Lert.

	£
Variable costs per unit	
Direct materials	2.00
Direct labour	3.00
Manufacturing royalties	0.50
Fixed costs per unit	2.75

Calculate the contribution made by the sale of one unit of Lert.

Answer:

Selling price – Variable costs = Contribution
   £10   –   £5.50   =   £4.50

Marginal costing is used in a variety of situations. The following are examined at A2.

Make or buy decisions

Example:

Reena manufactures saris. Her estimated costs and revenues for the next financial year are shown:

Costs and revenues per sari based on production of 500 saris

	£
Selling price	35
Direct material	8
Direct labour	4
Fixed costs	12
Profit per sari	11

Total profit for the year = £5500.

An overseas manufacturer has offered to supply the same quality sari at a total cost of £15 per sari.

Reena believes that by maintaining the current selling price, she will increase her profits to £20 per sari, giving total profits of £10 000 per year.

Advise Reena whether, on financial grounds, she should accept the overseas manufacturer's offer.

Answer:

The offer should not be accepted. Contribution at present is £23. If the offer to purchase the saris is accepted, contribution will fall to £20.

The answer assumes that Reena could not profitably use elsewhere any resources that might be released by accepting the overseas offer. It also assumes that fixed costs are truly fixed — that any factory space not used cannot be sub-let thus producing additional income, and that any factory space vacated will not require additional costs (i.e. security, heating etc.).

Acceptance of additional work

Additional work undertaken at less than the usual selling price for the product should be considered provided there is spare capacity in the factory and that no 'regular' work is adversely affected. If the additional work yields a positive contribution, it should be accepted.

Remember that additional work does not need to cover any fixed costs since they will have been absorbed already into the costing (and therefore into the selling price of the regular work).

Example:

The Shackleton Manufacturing Company produces one product. The following information is available for the production of 10 000 units of the product.

Costs and revenues per unit	£
Direct materials	10
Direct labour	15
Fixed costs	8
Selling price	50

There is spare capacity in the factory. A retailer in New Zealand has indicated that she wishes to purchase 150 units of the product but that the maximum price that she is prepared to pay is £30. The retailer is prepared to pay all shipping and insurance costs.

Advise the managers of Shackleton whether they should accept the order from New Zealand.

Answer:

The order should be accepted. It will make a positive contribution of £5 per unit (£30 – £25) or a total contribution of £750.

Price setting

Once marginal costs have been established, they may be used to set the selling price to either regular customers or additional customers.

Example:

	£
Direct material costs per unit	17
Direct labour costs per unit	8
Manufacturing royalties	1
Total direct costs	26

Any percentage added to the total direct costs to determine a selling price to customers must be sufficient to cover all other costs (overheads incurred in all departments of the business) in getting the product into a saleable condition plus a profit mark-up that will enable the business to survive and prosper in the future.

The price charged to additional customers should not be lower than £26, i.e. any additional work must yield a positive contribution.

Optimum use of scarce resources

Businesses may be faced with a temporary shortage of one or more factors of production. There may be a shortage of particular raw materials or a particular skill in the work force. Any lack of these key factors of production will inevitably affect the business's ability to maximise profits.

Any long-term shortages must be resolved by changing to an alternative raw material or an alternative set of skilled workers.

Managers of a business faced with a temporary shortage of a resource must use the available resources in a way that maximises profits.

This is achieved by ensuring that each product using the scarce resource is ranked according to the contribution that the resource yields. Production is completed, as far as possible, in the best order of using the resource as calculated in the ranking.

Example:

Jack Close manufactures four products. Each product uses a 'defigh', a component imported from Bulgaria at a cost of £3 each. A series of industrial disputes has meant that only 20 000 defighs are available this year.

The following information is available for each product:

	AB/3 £	CD/4 £	EF/5 £	GH/6 £
Cost of component defigh	3	18	12	6
Other direct material costs	10	15	14	7
Direct labour costs	9	13	10	12
Fixed costs	12	14	7	9
Selling price	50	100	60	45
Profit	16	40	17	20
Maximum demand (units)	6000	2000	5000	4000

Calculate:

(a) the rank order of production necessary to maximise profits

(b) the number of each product to be manufactured that will maximise profits

Answer:

(a)

	AB/3	CD/4	EF/5	GH/6
Contribution per defigh	£28	£9	£6	£10
	(28/1)	(54/6)	(24/4)	(20/2)
Rank order of production	1	3	4	2

(b)

Number of defigh to be used	6000	6000	–	8000
Number of each product to be produced	6000	1000	–	4000

Absorption costing and marginal costing compared

A business can make its own rules with regard to inventory valuation when preparing financial statements for internal use. However, IAS 2 states that marginal costing techniques cannot be used to value inventories for use in published financial statements.

Absorption costing:
- Both direct costs and overhead costs are charged to the cost unit, so the profit earned by each unit can be determined.
- When a business requires an even production flow, profits will vary less using absorption costing than marginal costing.
- As output changes, total cost per unit changes as fixed costs are spread over a different number of units.
- Work-in-progress and inventories of finished goods include overheads and so are valued at production cost.

Marginal costing:
- is simple to apply to a product since the arbitrary apportionment of each overhead does not need to be made
- shows a constant net profit per unit when selling price is constant, even when output fluctuates
- appears to give the impression that overheads are unrelated to levels of production and that they are less important than direct costs
- emphasises contribution and this may result in prices being fixed so that fixed costs may not be adequately covered leading to lower profits (or even losses)
- avoids the problem of over- or under-absorption of overheads
- work-in-progress and inventories of finished goods cannot be calculated using marginal costing methods (IAS 2)

Calculation of break-even

Break-even occurs at the point where the level of output and/or sales yields neither a profit nor a loss. It represents the lowest level of sales revenue or units sold at which total revenue received is equal to total costs.

You must be able to calculate the break-even point. There are two methods required by the specification.

The unit contribution method

This is the simplest method to use. Contribution is more correctly termed 'contribution to fixed costs and profits'. If you can calculate contribution, it should not be difficult to determine how many of these contributions are needed to cover all the fixed costs (i.e. when the business or product breaks even). Remember that each sale of the product covers the variable costs incurred in the production of the product; only the fixed costs need to be covered by the contribution to break-even.

Example:

The following information relates to the products and sales of 'sorecs'.

	£
Direct material costs per unit	23
Direct labour costs per unit	17
Total fixed costs	65 000
Selling price per unit	60

Calculate the break-even point in units.

Answer:

Contribution per unit = £20 (60 – 23 – 17)

Break-even = $\dfrac{\text{Total fixed costs}}{\text{Contribution per unit}}$ = $\dfrac{65\ 000}{20}$ = 3250 units

It is recommended that you always write out any formula when you use it. This will help you to remember it. Also, if you get used to this practice, you are more likely to show the formula when answering an examination question. The examiner usually allocates 1 mark to the formula in questions requiring such a calculation. Notice the use of the words 'total' (total fixed costs) and 'per unit' (contribution per unit).

You could be asked to calculate the margin of safety. This indicates how far sales can fall before the business will fail to make a profit. It is the difference between sales (either actual or forecast) and the break-even point when actual or forecast sales are above the break-even point. In the previous example, forecast sales were 6000 sorecs, the break-even point was 3250 sorecs, therefore the margin of safety was 2750 units (6000 – 3250).

Examination questions often require you to determine the number of units to be sold to achieve a planned amount of profit. This can be calculated using the basic unit contribution method but adding the required profit to the fixed costs.

Example:

Henry requires a profit of £100 000. He supplies the following information:

	£
Selling price per unit	40
Variable costs per unit	21
Total fixed costs	50 000

Calculate the number of units to be sold that will achieve a profit of £100 000.

Answer:

Level of required sales = $\dfrac{\text{Total fixed costs + Target profits}}{\text{Contribution per unit}}$

$= \dfrac{£50\ 000 + £100\ 000}{19}$

= 7895 units (actually 7894.7368)

Notice that the required level of sales is always rounded up since it is unlikely that Henry could sell 0.7368 of a unit.

The contribution/sales ratio method

The unit contribution method can only be used to find the break-even point for a single product. The contribution/sales method should be used when there are a number of products being manufactured and sold or when the variable cost per unit and/or the selling price per unit is not available.

By contrast, this method expresses total contribution as a percentage or decimal fraction of total sales revenue. The resulting percentage or decimal fraction is divided into the total fixed costs.

Example:

The following marginal cost statement is prepared for Follows Ltd for the year ended 31 March 2010.

	£
Sales	370 000
Variable costs	125 000
Total contribution	245 000
Fixed costs	120 000
Profit for the year	125 000

Calculate the break-even level of sales revenue.

Answer:

Contribution to sales ratio $= \dfrac{245\ 000}{370\ 000} = 0.6622$

Break-even level of sales revenue $= \dfrac{120\ 000}{0.6622}$

$= £181\ 214$

Limitations of break-even graphs

Graphical means of determining break-even is no longer part of the specification. However, you should be able to explain the limitations of using graphical means to determine the break-even point for a product:
- There is an assumption that all data behave in a linear fashion.
- The break-even chart assumes that the only factor that affects cost and revenues is the volume of sales. In fact, costs and revenues can be affected by:
  - increases in output
  - changes in the economy
  - changes in technology etc.

- It is assumed that the capital–labour mix remains fixed.
- There is an assumption that all production is sold, i.e. there are no opening or closing inventories.
- They only show one product.

Activity based costing (ABC)

Activity based costing identifies the cost of each activity undertaken in a business. It seeks to assign costs to all products according to actual consumption, making the process much more objective.

Direct costs (materials and direct wages) are easily allocated to products. However, it is much more difficult to allocate overheads directly to products. ABC costing allocates as many overheads as possible as direct costs rather than apportioning them in some arbitrary way, as in the absorption costing model. This means that the costs of producing a product can be determined more precisely. This will enable the organisation to identify and then eliminate any products that prove to be unprofitable. If an area of high overheads is identified, managers can concentrate on methods of reducing the overheads. Alternatively, the selling price of the end product may be increased.

The traditional method of apportioning costs means that an organisation is often unable to determine accurately the actual costs of production. So managers may make decisions based on inaccurate data, especially when a multitude of products are being produced.

Two key terms are used in ABC:
- **Cost pools** draw together the indirect costs of an organisation. For example, a cost pool might be the depreciation of the manufacturing machinery. Once a cost pool has been identified a proportion of the pool must be apportioned to each cost centre. This requires a measure of the use of the indirect resource by each cost centre.
- **Cost drivers** provide the measure by which cost pools are apportioned. They are any functions or activities that cause costs to be incurred. In the example above, the cost driver would be the amount of time each product spends in the machine.

What are the benefits that a business hopes to derive from using activity based costing? It helps:
- to identify products that are profitable (or unprofitable)
- to identify efficient (or inefficient) departmental practices or efficient (or inefficient) activities
- to eliminate one product subsidising another
- to identify costs that may be incurred unnecessarily
- to control costs

What are the limitations of using activity based costing?

- There are still some overheads that cannot be allocated to a product.
- Not all activities consume resources in a linear manner, so the calculation of a cost driver may be at best difficult (or impossible) to calculate.

Standard costing

Standard costing sets levels of costs and revenues that ought to be achievable with reasonable levels of performance by workers and efficient working practices.

A plan of what should happen to individual direct material costs and direct labour costs is prepared along with a plan of what should happen to sales revenue. These plans are the standards to be achieved. When the actual costs are available, these are compared with the standards. Any differences are known as variances.

A variance is the difference between the standard cost/revenues and the actual cost/ revenues. Favourable variances increase predicted profits. Adverse variances reduce predicted profits.

You need to be able to calculate and interpret the following variances and their sub-variances.

Note: the prefix 'sub' is often omitted in the description of sub-variances.

Total direct materials variance identifies the difference between what a manager thought would be spent on direct materials (the standard) and the amount that was actually spent. The total direct material variance is divided into two sub-variances:

- Direct material price variance arises if there is a change in the price set in the standard and the price actually charged by the supplier of the direct materials. A favourable direct material price variance arises when the actual cost of purchasing the direct materials has fallen compared with the standard. An adverse direct material price variance arises when the actual cost of purchasing the direct materials has risen compared with the standard.
- Direct material usage variance arises if there is a change in the quantity that ought to have been used as set in the standard and the quantity actually used in manufacturing. A favourable direct material usage variance arises when fewer materials are actually used compared with the standard. An adverse direct material usage variance arises when more materials are actually used compared with the standard.

Total direct labour variance identifies the difference between what the manager thought would be used in the production process (the standard) and the amount that was actually used. The total direct labour variance is divided into two sub-variances:

- Direct labour efficiency variance arises when there is a change in the number of hours that ought to have been worked and the number of hours that were actually worked in the manufacturing process. A favourable direct labour efficiency variance arises when the number of hours actually worked is fewer than the standard set. An adverse direct labour efficiency variance arises when the number of hours actually worked is greater than the standard set.
- Direct labour rate variance arises if there is a change in the rate of pay set in the standard to the rate actually paid to direct labour. A favourable direct labour rate

variance arises when the wage rate actually paid is less than the standard wage rate set. An adverse direct labour rate variance arises when the wage rate actually paid is greater than the standard wage rate set.

You can calculate all variances identified in the specification by using the following grid.

Standard quantity × Standard price $\quad$ Sq × Sp $\left.\right\}$
$\qquad\qquad\qquad\qquad\qquad\qquad\qquad\qquad$ Materials usage variance

Actual quantity $\quad$ × Standard price $\quad$ Aq × Sp $\left.\right\}$
$\qquad\qquad\qquad\qquad\qquad\qquad\qquad\qquad$ Materials price variance

Actual quantity $\quad$ × Actual price $\quad\quad$ Aq × Ap

Sq × Sp $\left.\right\}$
$\qquad$ Labour efficiency variance

Aq × Sp $\left.\right\}$
$\qquad$ Labour rate variance

Aq × Ap

Sq × Sp $\left.\right\}$
$\qquad$ Sales volume variance

Aq × Sp $\left.\right\}$
$\qquad$ Sales price variance

Aq × Ap

Example:

The managers of Garstack Ltd provide the following information for February.

Standard costs:

Direct materials	720 kg at £14.00 per kg
Direct labour	230 hours at £9.50 per hour

Actual costs:

Direct materials	710 kg at £14.30 per kg
Direct labour	245 hours at £9.00 per hour

Calculate:

(a) the direct material usage sub-variance

(b) the direct material price sub-variance

(c) the total direct material variance

(d) the direct labour efficiency sub-variance

(e) the direct labour rate sub-variance

(f) the total direct labour variance

(g) the total direct expenses variance

Answer:

Sq × Sp   720 × £14.00 = 10 080

£140   favourable (a)

Aq × Sp   710 × £14.00 =   9 940

£213   adverse   (b)

Aq × Ap   710 × £14.30 = 10 153

£73   adverse   (c)

Sq × Sp   230 × £9.50   =   2 185.00

£142.50   adverse   (d)

Aq × Sp   245 × £9.50   =   2 327.50

£122.50   favourable (e)

Aq × Ap   245 × £9.00   =   2 205.00

£20.00   adverse   (f)

Total direct expenses variance = £93 adverse (g)

Standard costing aims to highlight areas of good practice in the production process. Any such areas may then be replicated in other sections of the business.

Standard costing will also reveal areas of the production process that could be improved and managers may then take actions to improve or remove the problems.

The identification of sub-variances focuses on prices and quantities used compared with the standards set. You will be aware through your studies that comparisons are only valid when comparing like with like. This principle also needs to be applied when using the grid to compare standard costs with actual costs.

The standard (or forecast) budget needs to be flexed (adjusted) in order to achieve the like with like comparison. Consider this example:

I wish to make 80 000 pairs of trainers. I think that this will use 5000 m² of leather and 1000 m² of other materials (these are my standard quantities).

I only make 60 000 pairs. How much leather and other materials would you expect me to use?

Clearly I should use much less leather and other materials. I should use 3750 m² of leather and 750 m² of other materials. These are the amounts that should be included in my standard grid to assess the efficiency of my use of materials.

Similarly, I think that I will use 3600 hours of direct labour to produce the 80 000 pairs of trainers. Making only 60 000 would mean that my workers should be able to complete these in 2700 hours.

You should always flex your budget if the actual output of the product is different to the standard set. Only flex the standard quantity of direct materials and the standard hours of direct labour.

Example:

The following information is given for the production of artificial Christmas trees.

Standard costs for 10 000 Christmas trees:

Direct materials	250 kg at £4.00 per kg
Direct labour	2000 hours at £8.50 per hour

Only 9000 Christmas trees were made and the actual costs were:

Direct materials	220 kg at £4.20 per kg
Direct labour	1850 hours at £8.20 per hour

Calculate:

(a) the direct material usage sub-variance

(b) the direct material price sub-variance

(c) the total direct material variance

(d) the direct labour efficiency sub-variance

(e) the direct labour rate sub-variance

(f) the total direct labour variance

(g) the total direct expenses variance

Answer:

Before using the figures in the grid, the standard quantities must be flexed so:

Standard quantity of materials that ought to be used is:

$$250 \times \frac{9000}{10\ 000} = 225\text{kg}$$

Standard labour hours that ought to have been spent are:

$$2000 \times \frac{9000}{10\ 000} = 1800 \text{ hours}$$

The grid looks like this:

Materials:

Sq × Sp   225 × £4.00 = £900

          £20   favourable material usage variance (a)

Aq × Sp   220 × £4.00 = £880

          £44   adverse material price variance   (b)

Aq × Ap   220 × £4.20 = £924

          £24   adverse total material variance   (c)

Labour:

Sq × Sp   1800 × £8.50 = £15 300

Aq × Sp   1850 × £8.50 = £15 725

Aq × Ap   1850 × £8.20 = £15 170

£425 adverse labour efficiency variance (d)

£555 favourable labour rate variance   (e)

£130 favourable total labour variance   (f)

Total direct expenses variance = £106 favourable (g).

Sales variances are not flexed. The figures given in the question are used in a similar way in the grid. But you must remember to ask yourself whether the business is better off (a favourable variance) or worse off (an adverse variance) when you calculate your answers.

Example:

Budgeted sales are 7500 at £20.

Actual sales were 8000 at £16.

Calculate:

(a) the sales volume sub-variance

(b) the sales price sub-variance

(c) the total sales variance

Answer:

Sq × Sp   7500 × £20 = £150 000

Aq × Sp   8000 × £20 = £160 000

Aq × Ap   8000 × £16 = £128 000

£10 000 favourable sales volume variance (a)

£32 000 adverse sales price variance   (b)

£22 000 adverse total sales variance   (c)

You should learn the grid and how to 'fit' the appropriate figures into it. You should also learn how to flex the budget. Remember, it is only the standard amounts that are flexed.

As well as mastering the calculations, you need to be able to suggest reasons why variances might have arisen. You should also be able to suggest reasons why the causes of one sub-variance may have influenced another sub-variance. This is a popular part of a question set on standard costing and will give you the chance to gain development marks.

For example, there may be an adverse materials usage variance and a favourable labour rate variance. The interrelationship might be that more materials have been used because cheaper labour has been employed; the lower cost labour may be unskilled and they therefore make more mistakes, leading to more materials being used.

You may be asked to prepare a reconciliation statement using the variances either given in the question or calculated in an earlier part of the question. This could be reconciling budgeted profit with actual profit or budgeted costs with actual costs.

Example:

The following variances have been calculated for the year ended 28 February 2010:

	£	
Materials usage variance	1700	adverse
Material price variance	800	favourable
Labour efficiency variance	750	favourable
Labour rate variance	300	adverse

The budgeted profit for the year ended 28 February 2010 is expected to be £210 000.

Prepare a statement to calculate the actual profit for the year ended 28 February 2010.

Answer:

	£
Budgeted profit for the year	210 000
Materials usage variance	(1 700)
Materials price variance	800
Labour efficiency variance	750
Labour rate variance	(300)
Actual profit for the year	209 550

Capital investment appraisal

Capital expenditure is spending on purchasing non-current assets or improving them. Normal maintenance or repairs are revenue expenditure and are shown on the business income statement

Generally, capital projects involve the commitment of large sums of money that will be tied up for a considerable amount of time. It is therefore important that business managers get good value for the money spent.

Capital projects are appraised (evaluated) according to their future earning power in terms of either profits or cash flows or both.

Capital investment appraisal only considers incremental revenues and incremental expenditure — that is, the difference that undertaking the investment will make. So only additional revenue and additional expenditure caused by the investment is considered.

You need to know, understand and be able to calculate payback and net present value (NPV) methods of capital investment appraisal.

Payback

Payback considers the amount of time that it will take for the investment to cover its total cost.

This method is widely used in practice since most businesses are concerned with short time horizons — the sooner the initial outlay is recouped the better. A long time horizon is clearly more risky — longer time periods make forecasts less reliable.

Payback is fairly simple to calculate and understand: it uses cash flows so is regarded as being more objective than using profits; it shows the investment that involves the least risk (i.e. the shortest time to cover the initial outlay); it shows the investment that protects the liquidity of the business best.

However, it does not consider cash flows that occur in the years after payback, nor does it take into account differing patterns of cash flows.

Although a criticism of payback is that it does not generally take into account the time value of money, this can be easily overcome by using discounting techniques.

Example:

The managers of Nosirrah Ltd wish to purchase one new machine. The following information is given for the two models that are under consideration.

	Model A	Model B
	£	£
Initial cost	210 000	300 000
Net cash flows		
Year 1	50 000	150 000
Year 2	75 000	150 000
Year 3	85 000	150 000

(a) Calculate the payback period for each machine.

(b) State which machine the managers should purchase.

Answer:

(a) Model A = 3 years; model B = 2 years

(b) Machine B

In order to overcome the criticism that payback does not take into account the time value of money, the discounted payback method may be used. The annual net cash flows are discounted using the business's current cost of capital.

Example:

The managers of Ardnas plc are considering the purchase of a new machine costing £250 000. The machine is expected to produce goods for the next 5 years. The net cash flows accrue evenly throughout the year.

The net cash flows are shown:

	£
Year 1	65 000
Year 2	68 000
Year 3	72 000
Year 4	77 000
Year 5	83 000

The current cost of capital for Ardnas plc is 8%.

An extract from the present value table for £1 at 8% per annum is shown:

Year	8%
Year 1	£0.926
Year 2	£0.857
Year 3	£0.794
Year 4	£0.735
Year 5	£0.681

Calculate the discounted payback period for the new machine.

Answer:

	Net cash flow £	Discounting factor	Net present value £
Year 0	(250 000)	1	(250 000)
Year 1	65 000	0.926	60 190
Year 2	68 000	0.857	58 276
Year 3	72 000	0.794	57 168
Year 4	77 000	0.735	56 595
Year 5	83 000	0.681	56 523

Payback will be part way through year 5.

£250 000 – (60 190 + 58 276 + 57 168 + 56 595) = 17 771

$\dfrac{17\ 771}{56\ 523} = 0.3144$

Therefore payback is 5.31 years.

Net present value method

The net present value method also recognises the time value of money. The method compares the present-day value of estimated future net cash flows with the initial cost of the investment. If the result is positive, the investment should be considered. If the result is negative, the investment should not be undertaken.

Note that both methods use cash flows not profits. If profits are given in the question, then any non-cash flows used in the income statement must be 'added back' to the profit in order to determine cash flows.

Example:

Rachel is considering whether she should purchase a new lathe for her workshop. The lathe will cost £14 000. It will be used for 5 years then will be sold for £500 as scrap.

The following cash flows relate to the lathe:

Year	Revenue receipts £	Revenue expenditure £
1	10 000	6 000
2	12 000	6 000
3	14 000	7 000
4	17 000	8 000
5	15 000	9 000

Rachel's current cost of capital is 9%.

All cash flows arise at the end of the relevant year.

An extract from the present value table for £1 at 9% per annum is given:

Year	9%
1	0.917
2	0.842
3	0.772
4	0.708
5	0.650

Calculate the NPV for the new lathe and advise Rachel if the lathe should be purchased.

Answer:

Year	Net cash flow £	Discount factor	Net present value £
0	(14 000)	1	(14 000)
1	4 000	0.917	3 668
2	6 000	0.842	5 052
3	7 000	0.772	5 404
4	9 000	0.708	6 372
5	6 500	0.650	4 225
		Net present value	10 721

The new lathe should be purchased. It gives a positive net present value of £10 721.

If more than one investment is being considered, the NPV of each investment is calculated and the one that yields the greatest NPV should be chosen.

This type of question is often linked to an evaluative conclusion and may also contain a social accounting dilemma (see page 46).

Budgets and budgetary control

CIMA defines a budget as a 'plan expressed in money'. It is prepared well ahead of the period of time under review. The budget generally shows the income that it is hoped will be generated and the expenditure that is likely to be incurred.

Budgets are based on the objectives of the business and should show the likely outcomes of the policies to be pursued.

Budgetary control delegates financial planning to managers and makes them responsible for the implementation of policy designed to achieve the objectives of the business as a whole.

The actual performance of managers and their departments is continually compared against the results that have been planned in the departmental budgets. This continuous evaluation of departmental performance allows appraisal to ensure that the business objectives are being achieved or allows remedial action to be implemented. It also ensures that all departmental decision making is in line with the overall corporate plan.

Two of the functions of budgeting are planning and control. Senior managers prepare a strategic plan that identifies long-term objectives for the business. More detailed operational departmental plans are needed to ensure that the long-term objectives are achievable and ultimately achieved. The individual departments are controlled by the implementation of their own individual budget.

Each departmental budget will contribute to the master budget. The departmental budgets are drawn together into a master budget. This is really a budgeted set of financial statements prepared for the budget period. Once the master budget has been agreed, it can be scrutinised to see if each contributing budget is as planned; if not, an investigation will be conducted to discover the reasons for the deviations. This process ensures that departmental decisions reflect the overall objectives of the business.

Preparing budgets

You should be able to prepare and comment on purchases, sales, production, labour, debtor and creditor budgets and their relationship with the master budget. You could also be asked to prepare a cash budget as part of the synoptic element from ACCN2.

Debtor, creditor and cash budgets

The format of most budgets follows the same pattern:

	Debtor budget	**Creditor budget**	**Cash budget**
Opening balance	Opening debtors	Opening creditors	Opening bank balance
Plus increases	Credit sales	Credit purchases	Receipts
Less decreases	Cash received	Cash payments	Payments made
Closing balance	Closing debtors	Closing creditors	Closing bank balance

Although cash budgets are not mentioned specifically in the A2 specification, you should revise how they are produced. They could be examined as part of the synoptic assessment.

The budgets that use a slightly different format are the sales budget, the production and purchases budget, and the labour budget.

Sales budget

The sales budget is generally the first budget to be prepared because most businesses are sales driven. It is also one of the most difficult to prepare since forecasting future customers' demands is generally beyond a supplier's control.

An examination question could ask you to prepare a sales budget either in sales units or in sales value.

An example of both is shown:

	April	**May**	**June**
Budgeted sales in units	2100	2200	2300
Budgeted sales at £3.70 per unit	£7770	£8140	£8510

Production and purchases budgets

A production budget forecasts the levels of production that will be necessary to satisfy the forecast level of sales. It shows the quantity of finished goods that need to be produced to meet expected sales plus the inventory needed at the end of each budget period.

A purchases budget forecasts the levels of purchases that need to be acquired in order to satisfy the forecast level of sales. It shows how many purchases need to be made to meet expected sales plus the inventory needed at the end of each budget period.

Example 1 Production budget:

Haria & Co. supply the following budgeted sales figures:

	October £000	**November** £000	**December** £000	**January** £000
Budgeted sales	95	105	110	80

It is policy to maintain inventory levels at 20% of the following month's budgeted sales.

Prepare a production budget for the 3 months ending 31 December.

Answer:

The opening inventory in October   should be £19 000 (95 000 × 20%)

The opening inventory in November should be £21 000 (105 000 × 20%)

The opening inventory in December should be £22 000 (110 000 × 20%)

The closing inventory   in December should be £16 000 (80 000 × 20%)

Production budget:

	October £000	November £000	December £000
Budgeted sales	95	105	110
Closing inventory	21	22	16
	116	127	126
Opening inventory	19	21	22
Production needed	97	106	104

Example 2 Purchases budget:

Haria & Co. supply the following budgeted sales figures:

	October £000	November £000	December £000	January £000
Budgeted sales	95	105	110	80

It is policy to maintain inventory levels at 20% of the following month's budgeted sales.

Prepare a purchases budget...

Your answer should look very similar to the previous example. The only differences are the heading and the final line of the budget, which should read 'Purchases required'.

Although the format is slightly different to the norm, talk yourself through this layout and you will see how logical it is.

In October, Haria needed £95 000 goods to satisfy customers and they needed £21 000 of inventory. So altogether the requirement was £116 000 goods. But they already had £19 000 worth left over from last month, so only £97 000 needed to be produced (or purchased).

Labour budgets

A labour budget is prepared to determine the business's need for labour in the future. It can be prepared in hours of labour required and/or numbers of workers required.

Example:

Hugo provided the following production budget.

	August	September	October	November
Production (units)	10 000	12 000	11 000	9 500

Each unit of production required 2 hours of labour. Hugo has 22 000 hours of labour available each month. Each worker works a 40-hour week.

Prepare a labour budget for the 4 months ending 30 November.

Answer:

	August	September	October	November
Labour requirement	20 000 hours	24 000 hours	22 000 hours	19 000 hours
Surplus hours	2000 hours	–	–	–
Shortfall hours	–	2000 hours	–	3000 hours
Surplus labour	50 workers	–	–	–
Labour deficit	–	50 workers	–	75 workers

The budget shows that in September and November Hugo requires extra staff and that in August he has surplus labour.

In August, workers will need to be laid off or moved to an alternative part of the production process. In September and November, further staff need to be employed, possibly on a part-time or temporary basis since the deficits do not occur each month.

Budgeted balance sheets and income statements

Although you will not be required to prepare a detailed master budget as part of an examination question, you could be asked to prepare a summarised budgeted income statement and budgeted balance sheet from a cash budget.

This will test your ability to apply the accruals concept; it will also test your ability to differentiate between capital and revenue expenditure and to distinguish cash from non-cash expenses.

Note the following important points:
- Actual sales and purchases for each month may be given and so will be included in the budgeted income statement for those months. However, payments from credit customers and to credit suppliers may be paid in later months and should be included in the cash budgets for those later months.
- This principle also applies to expenses payments. For example, if rent is £300 per month, this amount should be included in the budgeted income statement whether

it is paid or not. The payment should only be included in the month(s) when the amount is actually paid.

- Depreciation of any non-current asset should be included in the budgeted income statement using the appropriate amount. For example, depreciation of £12 000 means £3000 to be included for a budgeted income statement covering 3 months.
- A provision for doubtful debts appears in a budgeted income statement but not in a cash budget.

A few final points to remember:

The budgeted income statement heading should be as follows:

**Tom Smith. Budgeted income statement for the 3 months ending
31 December 2010**

The above would be a perfect heading. Notice that your heading should:

- contain the name of the business
- contain the words 'budgeted' and 'ending'
- not show any abbreviations

Remember that the budgeted income statement should show the totals for the time period for each item included. It should *not* show individual monthly figures (remember also that any budgets you prepare *should* be shown month by month).

For those of you studying business studies, many business studies texts and teachers refer to 'cash budgets' as 'cash flow forecasts'. Remember that these are the same thing.

Social accounting

Social and ethical factors

Many questions, especially costing questions and questions involving capital investment appraisal, introduce factors that could negatively affect the stakeholders of a business (employees, the local and national economy, the environment). A consideration of social and ethical factors could form part of such a question. You must be aware of some of these factors and be able to discuss them sensibly.

Most teenagers are aware of many issues that affect stakeholders and can discuss them in great depth. However, any discussion must be focused and you must not go off the topic at a tangent that you may feel is important. There seems to be more of a danger in written rather than numerical answers for candidates to lose focus on the precise question set and to spend time discussing irrelevant factors. This can lead to candidates spending too much time on this part of a question.

Look at the number of marks allocated to this part of the question and multiply it by 1.3 minutes. So 13 minutes should be devoted to a 10-mark question; around 20 minutes should be taken to acquire 15 marks, and so on. This simple calculation will help you to avoid overrunning the time that should be allocated to a particular part of a question. Use your watch. Before you start writing your answer, draft a brief plan so that you cover a number of points and do not repeat or labour any one of them.

Remember to reach a judgement if a question requires you to evaluate, for example, alternative courses of action. Also remember that you must reach a conclusion when the instruction 'discuss' is part of the question.

In this section of the guide there are ten questions. Each question is followed by two sample answers interspersed with comments from the examiner.

The questions are typical of those you could be faced with in your A2 examination. Some of the questions will test your ability to solve numerical problems using knowledge, understanding and application skills. Others will involve some analysis and then an evaluation of a scenario.

Sample answers

In each case, the first answer (by candidate A) is intended to show the type of response that would earn a grade A. Remember that a grade-A response does not mean that the answer is perfect. You will see that there is a range of marks that could score a grade A.

The answers given by candidate B illustrate the types of errors that weaker candidates tend to make, thus depriving them of vital marks that could so easily have moved their script up into another grade boundary.

In the sample answers, each point awarded a mark is shown with a tick ✓. Where you see ✓*, this indicates that the mark has been awarded for the candidate's own figure, i.e. although the final figure is incorrect it is based on the correct method.

Resist the temptation to look at these answers before you attempt the question.

Examiner comments

The examiner comments are preceded by the icon $\mathcal{e}$. In some cases they are shown within the candidate's answer, but in the main they appear after the candidate's answer. In weaker answers, the comments point out areas for improvement and some of the common errors found in answers that are near to the pass/fail boundary.

Manufacturing accounts

Donna K. Babbe provides the following information for her manufacturing business for the year ended 31 December 2009.

She transfers goods from the manufacturing account to the income statement at cost plus 40%.

	£
Sales	3 170 500
Purchases of raw materials	287 460
Returns inwards	490
Returns outwards	880
Carriage inwards	1 260
Carriage outwards	2 010
Manufacturing royalties	6 250
Wages	640 000
Insurances	18 140
General factory overheads	157 636
Factory machinery at cost	600 000
Office equipment at cost	120 000
Vehicles at cost	580 000

Additional information

Inventories at 31 December

	2008	2009
Raw materials	12 400	13 200
Work-in-progress	9 780	11 400
Finished goods valued at transfer prices	25 480	28 560

(1) Manufacturing royalties paid in advance amounted to £750.

(2) Insurance paid in advance amounted to £1200. Sixty per cent of insurance costs are to be charged to the manufacturing account and the remainder is to be charged to the income statement.

(3) Wages accrued and unpaid amounted to £14 000. Wage costs are 80% for factory workers, with the remainder for sales distribution and administrative staff. Factory wages are 70% for direct labour, with the remainder paid to factory supervisory staff.

(4) Depreciation is to be provided on all non-current assets at 10% per annum on cost.

REQUIRED

Prepare a manufacturing account for the year ended 31 December 2009.

(22 marks)

plus 2 marks for quality of presentation

Answer to question 1: candidate A

D. K. Babbe: *Manufacturing account for the year ended 31 December 2009*

	£	£
Inventory		12 400
Purchases of materials		287 460 ✓
Carriage inwards		1 260 ✓
Returns out		880 ✓
		300 240
Inventory		(13 200) ✓
Raw materials used		287 040 ✓
Manufacturing wages		366 240 ✓ ✓ ✓ ✓
Royalties		5 500 ✓
Prime cost		658 780 ✓
Factory overheads		
Insurances	10 884	
General overheads	157 636 ✓	
Indirect wages	156 960 ✓	
Depreciation	130 000	445 480
		1 114 260
Work-in-progress adjustment		1 620
Total production cost		1 115 880 ✓*
Manufacturing profit		446 352 ✓*
Transfer price		1 562 232 ✓*

The quality of presentation marks are awarded for the descriptions 'raw materials used', 'prime cost', 'total production cost' and 'transfer price'.

The manufacturing account has a good, clear heading. It is written out in full and does not contain any abbreviations. The layout is good. The candidate has not shown any workings and this might have cost marks, especially for the calculations of manufacturing and indirect wages. As it happens, both are correct so score the allocated marks. However, lack of workings to show how the insurance figure is arrived at has cost a couple of marks. A careless error has been made — the candidate has calculated depreciation on all non-current assets rather than just factory machinery. The work-in-progress adjustment has been calculated correctly but the candidate has added it when it should have been deducted. The candidate scores 'own figure' marks for the total production cost, manufacturing profit and transfer price.

Overall, 16 marks are awarded for the account plus 2 presentation marks, giving a total of 18 out of a possible 24 marks. This is a grade-A answer.

Answer to question 1: candidate B

Manuf a/c for the y/e 31 Dec 09

Sales			3 170 500
Rets out			880
			3 169 620
Inventory		12 400	
Raw materials		287 460 ✓	
		299 860	
		13 200 ✓	
		286 660	
Wages		654 000 ✓	(640 000 + 14 000)
		940 660	
Less overheads			
Royalties	5 500	(6250 – 750)	
Insurance	16 940 ✓	(18 140 – 1200)	
General overheads	157 636 ✓		
Depreciation	60 000 ✓	240 076	
		700 584	
WIP		9 780 ✓	
		710 364	
WIP		11 400 ✓	
		698 964 ✓*	
Profit		978 549.60	
Transfer price		1 677 513.60 ✓*	

None of the quality of presentation marks is scored. The heading is incomplete, the business name is missing and the use of abbreviations precludes marks from being awarded. The only 'key' description used is transfer price. Prime cost should be identified to gain the 'own figure' mark.

Manufacturing accounts are merely a list of the costs of running a factory to produce goods and should not include sales. Although the prime cost section is incomplete, it does score 3 marks. It is good to see that the candidate has included workings for wages and insurance; without the workings, 2 marks would have been forfeited. The royalties calculation is correct and is supported by workings, but the amount should have contributed to prime cost. The candidate has deducted the factory overheads from prime cost and so scores only half the available marks. This is a common mistake that can be avoided by remembering that a manufacturing account lists the 'ingredient' costs that go towards the total costs of producing the products. The WIP adjustment is completed accurately. The manufacturing profit has been calculated at 140%, which in reality should have been the candidate's 'own' transfer price.

Although this is not a good attempt by an A2 candidate, 10 marks have been gained, which is enough to earn a marginal grade E.

Question 2

Provision for unrealised profit

The following information is provided for Rishta plc, a manufacturing company.

It is company policy to transfer goods from the manufacturing account to the income statement at cost plus 35%.

Inventories at 30 November

	2008	2009
	£	£
Raw materials	60 400	63 200
Work-in-progress	32 780	34 900
Finished goods valued at transfer price	114 750	121 500

	£
Sales	2 450 000
Total production costs	972 000

REQUIRED

(a) Calculate the transfer price of goods manufactured for inclusion in an income statement. (3 marks)

(b) Prepare an extract from the income statement for the year ended 30 November 2009, showing clearly the gross profit on trading activities. (6 marks)

(c) Prepare a provision for unrealised profit account for the year ended 30 November 2009. (8 marks)

(d) Prepare an extract from the income statement for the year ended 30 November 2009 showing total gross profit and the treatment of the provision for unrealised profit. (4 marks)

(e) Prepare an extract from the balance sheet at 30 November 2009 showing the treatment of inventories. (4 marks)

(f) Explain why Rishta plc needs to prepare a provision for unrealised profit. (5 marks)

■ ■ ■

Answer to question 2: candidate A

(a) Transfer price = £1 312 200 ✓ ✓ ✓

> No workings have been provided so a minor slip by the candidate would have meant no marks. You should always show detailed workings. Even the best candidates sometimes make errors under the pressure of the examination.

(b) *Rishta plc: Income statement extract for the year ended 30 November 09*

	£	£
Sales		2 450 000 ✓
Less cost of sales		
Inventory 1 December 2008	114 750 ✓	
Transfer price of finished goods	1 312 000	
	1 426 750	
Inventory 30 November 2009	121 500 ✓	1 305 250
Gross profit		1 144 750 ✓*

This answer is laid out well and scores 4 marks. Unfortunately, it is marred by two errors: the use of 09 in the date, and the careless use of £1 312 000 instead of the amount calculated in part (a) — £1 312 200. Care must be taken in every part of an answer. The examiner cannot reward work if it is not accurate.

(c) *Provision for unrealised profit*

		1 December 2008 Balance b/d	29 750 ✓ ✓ ✓ w1
30 November 2009 Balance c/d	31 500 ✓ ✓ ✓ w2	Income statement	1 750 ✓
	31 500		31 500
	31 500	1 December 2009 Balance b/d	31 500 ✓

w1 $114\ 750 \times \dfrac{35}{135} = 29\ 750$ w2 $121\ 500 \times \dfrac{35}{135} = 31\ 500$

This answer scores full marks. The amount of unrealised profit contained in the inventory valuation at both year ends has been calculated accurately and is supported by detailed workings. The account is written out neatly and the amount transferred to the income statement has been calculated and labelled correctly.

(d) *Income statement extract for the year ended 30 November 2009*

	£	£	
Gross profit on trading		1 144 750 ✓*	
Gross profit on manufacturing	340 200 ✓		1 312 200 – 972 000
Provision for unrealised profit	1 750 ✓	338 450	
Total gross profit		1 483 300 ✓*	

This is another perfect answer. The candidate has used the correct gross profit on manufacturing despite a slip in part (a) of the answer. It is good to see this figure being backed up by workings rather than trusting the accurate use of a calculator.

(e)

Balance sheet extract at 30 November 2009 ✓

Current assets	£
Inventories	
Raw materials	63 200
Work-in-progress	34 900
Finished goods	90 000 ✓ ✓
	188 100 ✓

📝 A 'safer' answer might have shown the workings for the cost price of the finished goods, e.g.

Finished goods	£121 500
Less provision for unrealised profit	£31 500
	£90 000

However, this answer is again completely correct.

(f) A provision for unrealised profit is necessary to reduce the value of inventories of finished goods back to cost price. ✓ If Rishta didn't do this, its profits would be inflated ✓ by the amount of the increase in the provision over the year ✓. The value of the inventory in the balance sheet would also be inflated ✓, so the value of inventories should always be shown at cost price.

📝 The candidate could have mentioned prudence and the IAS 2 inventories standard, and could have referred to realisation of profits and that the inventories given in the question actually contain 'unrealised profit'.

📝 **Overall this candidate's answer is a comfortable grade A, scoring 27 out of a possible 30 marks.**

■ ■ ■

Answer to question 2: candidate B

(a) 972 000 ✓ × 35% = 340 200 ✓*

📝 The candidate has used 35% to calculate the transfer price. The result is, in fact, the manufacturing profit. If the candidate had added this to the production cost, the correct answer would have been achieved.

(b)

	£	£	
Sales		2 450 000 ✓	
Inventory	3 278		(114 750 ÷ 35)
Transfer price	340 200 ✓*		
	343 478		
Inventory	3 471	340 007	(121 500 ÷ 35)
GP		2 109 993	

🖉 Only 2 marks are scored here. The candidate has failed to score the mark allocated for a heading. All answers should have a clear heading. A mark is not always on offer for headings, but the only way to ensure you are rewarded for headings that do carry a mark is to use a heading for every answer. It is good to see an attempt to show workings, although the inventories of finished goods should have been included as shown in the question. An incorrect figure was used for the transfer price but it is rewarded as the candidate used his or her own figure as calculated in part (a). Although the gross profit is correct using the candidate's own figures, it is not awarded a mark because the description 'Gross profit' is not written in full.

(c)

Prov for unreal profit

		Bal b/d	3 278
Bal c/d	3 471	Inc Stat	193 ✓
	3 471		3 471
		Bal b/d	3 471 ✓*

🖉 This answer scores 2 marks. The candidate has not used the unrealised profit included in the inventory valuations. The candidate's 'own' inventory was used. However, two principle marks are awarded: one for the balancing figure transferred to the income statement, and the other for correctly bringing the balance down. Always bring the balances down into the new time period. If this is not done the account is incomplete.

(d)

Gross profit on trading	2 109 993 ✓*
Gross profit on manufacturing	631 800
Total gross profit	2 741 793
Provision for unrealised profit	193
	2 741 600 ✓*

🖉 Candidate B scores 2 marks for this answer. The marks are for total gross profit and for one of its components. The candidate has failed to gain the mark for provision for unrealised profit. It was not deducted from the manufacturing profit (2 marks). As before, the answer should have had a heading.

(e)

	£	£
Inventories of raw materials		63 200
Work in progress		34 900
Finished goods	3 471 ✓*	
Provision for unr profits	3 471 ✓*	0
		98 100 ✓*

🖉 The candidate has chosen his or her own closing inventory of finished goods and his or her own balance from the provision account; both figures are correct in principle. Three out of the 4 marks available are awarded.

(f) Rishta plc needs to prepare a provision for unrealised profit because the laws of IASs say that they must so that the financial statements show a fair and true report.

> There is nothing of value in this answer. The candidate has merely repeated phrases that he or she has read or heard a teacher mention. This is a poor effort from an A2 candidate.

> **Overall, the candidate has shown that with a little more care and diligence he or she could have scored a marginal E grade. However, with the answers submitted, the candidate has scored a total of 11 out of a possible 30 marks — a marginal fail.**

Question 3

Absorption costing

The Destonds Manufacturing Company has three production departments and two service departments. The following information relates to each department *after* all costs have been allocated or apportioned:

	Production departments			Service departments	
	A	**B**	**C**	**Maintenance**	**Canteen**
	£	£	£	£	£
Budgeted total overhead costs	160 000	180 000	90 000	120 000	110 000
Budgeted total labour hours worked	48 000	6 000	700		
Budgeted total machine hours worked	3 000	21 000	10 000		

The service department costs are to be apportioned as follows:

	A	**B**	**C**	**Maintenance**	**Canteen**
Maintenance	35%	30%	25%		10%
Canteen	20%	15%	35%	30%	

REQUIRED

(a) Prepare a statement to show how the costs of the service departments are re-apportioned between the production departments. (12 marks)

(b) Calculate the overhead absorption rate for each production department. State the basis used, giving a reason for your choice of basis. (12 marks)

Management has been asked to cost Job 12748/BU. The job would require:

7 kilograms of materials costing £7.50 per kilogram

5 hours of direct labour at £9.50 per hour

It would spend 2 hours in department A, 3 hours in department B and 30 minutes in department C.

The job would be marked up by 60%.

REQUIRED

(c) Prepare a statement to show how the management would cost the job. (8 marks)

(d) Discuss the advantages of using absorption costing compared to marginal costing. (8 marks)

Answer to question 3: candidate A

(a)

	A	B	C	Maintenance	Canteen
	£	£	£	£	£
Total overhead costs	160 000	180 000	90 000	120 000	110 000
Maintenance	42 000 ✓	36 000 ✓	30 000 ✓	(120 000) ✓	12 000 ✓
	202 000	216 000	120 000	–	122 000
Canteen	22 400	16 800	39 200	33 600	(122 000) ✓
	224 400 ✓*	232 800 ✓*	159 200 ✓* closed down so ignored	–

> 🖉 This answer is laid out clearly with neat and, in the main, accurate calculations. The candidate obviously knows the theory. Only the transfer of the canteen costs was miscalculated by the inclusion of the maintenance department, which had already been apportioned. This answer scores 9 marks.

(b)

Dept A $\dfrac{224\ 400\ ✓*}{48\ 000\ ✓}$ = £4.675 ✓* per labour hour

Dept B $\dfrac{232\ 800\ ✓*}{21\ 000\ ✓}$ = 11.0857 ✓* per machine hour

Dept C $\dfrac{159\ 200\ ✓*}{10\ 000\ ✓}$ = £15.92 ✓* per machine hour

> 🖉 Candidate A scores 9 marks for this answer. This is another good, accurate answer that correctly uses the candidate's own total from part (a). The one slip that has been made is that no reason is given for the choice of basis. Is this because the candidate did not read the question carefully enough or because the answer has been rushed?

(c)

Job 12748/BU

	£
Material costs	52.50 ✓
Direct labour costs	47.50 ✓
Overheads A	9.35 ✓*
B	33.26 ✓*
C	7.69
Total cost	150.30 ✓*
Profit	90.18 ✓*
Selling price	240.48 ✓*

> 🖉 Candidate A scores 7 marks. The job is costed accurately with the exception of department C's overheads where the overheads to be absorbed should have been £7.96. The candidate has made a transposition error.

(d) Both methods of costing look at the effect that overheads have on costs. Absorption costing includes overheads ✓ whereas marginal costing ignores them. ✓

> This is a reasonable opening, showing that the candidate is aware of the impact that overheads have on the costing process.

The main advantage that absorption costing has is that all costs are recovered by being included in the selling price. ✓ A good example is when costing job 12748/BU you can see that every cost and profit is included in working out the selling price. ✓ Marginal costing does not attempt to allocate any overheads to a product — they are period costs. ✓

> The candidate identifies an advantage and develops the point well. Knowledge is applied to the question.

Conclusion. Absorption costing has to be included if you want to cover all the costs involved in manufacturing, so in the long term absorption costs should be used. Marginal costing is used for specialised costing, such as a one-off contract, or to see the best combination of products if there is a shortage of direct costs. ✓ ✓ You couldn't use marginal costing to cost out every piece of production — you would never cover all your overheads.

> Discussions require a summing up, drawing the major points together. It is good to see that the candidate has done this. He or she has repeated the need to cover all costs in the long run and has shown understanding of the specialised uses of marginal costing. Candidate A scores 7 marks for this part.

> **Overall this is a sound answer. The few minor errors have not precluded the candidate from gaining sufficient marks to achieve a grade A. A total of 32 out of a possible 40 marks are scored.**

■ ■ ■

Answer to question 3: candidate B

(a)

	A	B	C	Main	Cant
Total overheads	160 000	180 000	90 000	120 000	110 000
30% × 120 000	36 000	36 000 ✓	36 000		36 000
	196 000	216 000	126 000		146 000
10% × 146 000	14 600	14 600	14 600		
	210 600 ✓*	230 600 ✓*	140 600 ✓*		

> Candidate B has a vague idea that totals are needed for the production departments and has used 30% and 10% as the basis for apportioning the overheads for the service departments. Only the total overheads for the production departments scores own figure marks. It is good to see some attempt at workings, although they are completely off the point. Candidate B scores 4 marks.

(b)

A $\dfrac{210\ 600}{48\ 000}$ ✓* $= £4.3875$ ✓* $\dfrac{210\ 600}{3000}$ $= £70.20$

B $\dfrac{230\ 600}{6000}$ $= £38.433$ $\dfrac{230\ 600}{21\ 000}$ ✓* $= £10.981$ ✓*

C $\dfrac{140\ 600}{700}$ $= £200.857$ $\dfrac{140\ 600}{10\ 000}$ ✓* $= £14.06$ ✓*

This answer scores 9 marks. The candidate is hedging his or her bets by calculating both labour hours and machine hours for absorbing the departmental overheads. The candidate scores the three answers that are correct using his or her own figures but clearly there is confusion with regard to the process involved.

(c)

Materials		52.50 ✓	
Wages		47.50 ✓	
Overheads	A	74.5875	4.38750 + 70.20
	B	49.414	38.433 + 10.981
	C	214.917	200.857 + 14.06
		438.9185	
		263.3511 ✓*	
Selling price		706.2696 ✓*	

Candidate B scores 4 marks for this answer. He or she has used all the information calculated in part (b). Since there are extraneous items included, there can be no own figure mark for the total cost. Again, there is a good use of workings (sadly, again, they are inaccurate so score no mark). The percentage mark up and selling price are correct using the candidate's own figures.

(d) Ran out of time.

This comment is superfluous. It is not surprising that the candidate ran out of time after doing double the work in answering part (b) of the question. You should only spend 1.33 minutes for each mark, so part (a) should require 16 minutes, part (b) 16 minutes and part (c) just over 10 minutes.

Overall candidate B has probably done just enough to scrape a grade E. A total of 17 marks have been scored out of a possible 40. With better allocation of time, a more comfortable pass grade might have been obtained.

Marginal costing

Wong Ltd manufactures three different products. The following budgeted information is available for the year ending 31 December 2010.

Marginal cost statements have been produced.

	A	B	C
Maximum demand (units)	70 000	20 000	30 000
Direct materials per unit	£10.00	£20.00	£30.00
Direct labour per unit	£4.00	£4.00	£6.00
Variable overheads per unit	£1.50	£1.75	£2.00
Fixed costs per unit	£0.80	£1.20	£2.10
Profit per unit	£3.70	£3.05	£4.90

The products are made with titarion, which costs £500 per kilogram.

There is a shortage of titarion used in the production processes. Wong Ltd is only able to acquire 250 000 kg for its production this year.

REQUIRED

(a) Calculate the rank order of production that would maximise profits. (9 marks)

(b) Calculate the number of each type of product to be manufactured that would maximise profits. (4 marks)

(c) Prepare a budgeted marginal cost statement showing total contribution and total profit for the year ending 31 December 2010 based on the optimum use of titarion. (12 marks)

(d) Calculate the level of sales revenue at which Wong Ltd will break even in the year ending 31 December 2010. (5 marks)

■ ■ ■

Answer to question 4. Candidate A

(a) Selling price

    A   10.00 + 4.00 + 1.50 + 0.80 + 3.70 = £20
    B   20 + 4 + 1.75 + 1.20 + 3.05 = £30
    C   30 + 6 + 2 + 2.10 + 4.90 = £45

Variable costs

    A   £15.50 contribution is £4.50 ✓
    B   £25.75 contribution is £4.25 ✓
    C   £38.00 contribution is £7.00 ✓

Amounts of metal in each

    A   2 kg
    B   4 kg
    C   6 kg

Contribution per kg   A   4.50 ÷ 2 = £2.25 ✓
                       B   4.25 ÷ 4 = £1.06 ✓
                       C   7.00 ÷ 6 = £1.17 ✓

So order of production is: A first ✓
                             C second ✓
                             B third ✓

> The full **9** marks are scored. This is a good, accurate answer, following a logical progression. Detailed workings are provided to support the correct answer. Showing such detailed workings means that if an error should occur, the candidate stands more chance of getting some marks.

(b) Wong Ltd would use 140 000 kg to produce 70 000 units of A. ✓ There would then be 110 000 kg left ✓ so they cannot produce all of C but they could use these to produce 18 333.33 units of C ✓, so they could produce 18 334 units of C.

> This is another good answer, which scores 3 marks. It contains a great deal of explanation and detail. Such detail must have taken a lot of time and this could lead to other answers being incomplete or another question remaining unfinished. The candidate has rounded up the units of C that could be produced. This could not happen as there is not enough material to complete 18 334 — there is only sufficient to fully complete 18 333 units of product A.

(c)   *Marginal cost statement*

                                                         £
Direct materials   (700 000 + 550 020)   1 250 020 ✓ ✓
Direct wages   (280 000 + 110 004)   390 004 ✓ ✓
Variable overheads   (105 000 + 36 668)   141 668 ✓ ✓
                                                  1 781 692
Fixed costs   (56 000 ✓ + 38 501 to nearest) 94 501
                                                  1 876 193
Expected profit   348 837 ✓*
Sales   (1 400 000 + 825 030)   2 225 030 ✓ ✓

> There is one error in this answer. The candidate has not taken into account the fundamental fact that fixed costs do not change with levels of activity and should total £143 000 (56 000 + 24 000 + 63 000). Otherwise, this is a good, neat answer that once again is supported by clear workings.

(d) Break-even for   A $\dfrac{\text{Total fixed costs}}{\text{Contribution per unit}}$ = $\dfrac{56\,000}{4.50}$ = 12 445 units of A

                          C $\dfrac{\text{Total fixed costs}}{\text{Contribution per unit}}$ = $\dfrac{38\,501}{7.00}$ = 5501 units of C

12 445 × £20 =   248 900
5501 × £45   =   247 545
                 £496 445   break-even sales revenue

⧉ This is a good, clear answer, but unfortunately it is totally incorrect. The candidate has tried to use the unit contribution method, which does not work for a multi-product set of figures. The candidate should have used the contribution to sales revenue method (C/S). Unfortunately, no marks can be awarded for this detailed calculation.

⧉ **Apart from part (d) candidate A has produced good, clear answers that are logical and easy to follow. Despite not scoring for part (d), this is a marginal grade-A answer. A total of 22 marks out of a possible 30 are scored.**

■ ■ ■

Answer to question 4: candidate B

(a) Make C first because it gives most profit, then A because it gives the next best profit and then if there is any titarion left make B because it gives the worst profit.

⧉ This answer follows the wrong approach completely and no marks can be awarded. The candidate has used the profit per unit as a basis for ranking the products. Contribution per unit of the scarce resource should have been used.

(b)

C	180 000 kg ✓	make 30 000 Cs ✓
A	70 000 kg ✓	make 35 000 As ✓
B	none left	0

⧉ This is an accurate answer using the candidate's own ranking from (a) and it scores 4 marks. The layout is rather spartan but the candidate clearly knows how to arrive at the allocation of a scarce resource.

(c)

Direct materials	1 250 000 ✓ ✓
Direct labour	800 000
Variable overheads	112 500 ✓ ✓
Fixed costs	91 000
	1 753 500
Profit	296 500 ✓*
Sales	2 050 000 ✓ ✓

⧉ This answer scores 7 marks. There are no workings to support any of the totals. The fact that the materials, variable overheads and the sales figures are correct using the candidate's own figures from (b) suggests that other marks could have been awarded if workings had been shown.

(d) 14% of 1 753 500 ✓ = £245 490 ✓*

⧉ The examiner cannot tell where the figures have come from and so cannot award part marks for the 14%—it should be 14.46%. Workings must always be shown.

⧉ **Overall, 13 marks are scored out of 30. This is sufficient to gain a marginal pass grade E.**

Question 5

Calculation of break-even

Blackstream Ltd manufactures one product. The following information is given for the two production departments for the year ended 31 December 2009. It is expected that **12 000 units** will be sold during the year.

	A	**B**
Direct machine hours	20 000 hours	5 000 hours
Direct labour hours	12 000 hours	10 000 hours

The overhead absorption rate for each department is:

Department **A** = £30.00 per machine hour
Department **B** = £8.60 per labour hour

The management of Blackstream Ltd calculates the selling price of one unit of the product based on production cost plus a 20% mark up.

The direct costs per unit are: 6 metres of materials at £7.00 per metre
2 hours of labour at £11.00 per hour

Each unit of production takes 1½ hours in department **A** and 2¼ hours in department **B**. All the overheads are fixed costs.

REQUIRED

(a) Calculate the selling price of one unit of the product. (6 marks)

(b) Calculate the number of units to be sold in the year to break even. (7 marks)

(c) Calculate the margin of safety as a percentage of expected demand (correct to one decimal place). (3 marks)

The workforce is currently in negotiation for a 10% pay rise.

REQUIRED

(d) Calculate the percentage change to the break-even position if the pay rise is implemented in full. (8 marks)

(e) Evaluate the usefulness of break-even analysis to the managers of Blackstream Ltd. (11 marks)

■ ■ ■

Answer to question 5: candidate A

(a) ***Selling price of the product***

Costs

Materials	(6 × 7)	42.00 ✓
Wages	(2 × 11)	22.00 ✓
Overheads	(1½ × 30) in A	45.00 ✓
	(2¼ × 8.60) in B	19.35 ✓
		128.35
Profit (20% × 128.35)		25.67 ✓
Selling price		154.02 ✓

✎ This is a good, accurate answer, which gains maximum marks. Each calculation is supported by clear workings.

(b)

Break-even = $\dfrac{\text{Total fixed costs}}{\text{Contribution per unit}}$ ✓

Total fixed costs 45.00
                   $\underline{19.35}$
                   64.35 × 12 000 = 772 200

Contribution   154.02 – 64.00 = 90.02
                   $\dfrac{772\,200}{90.02}$ ✓ ✓ ✓ = 8579 units ✓*

✎ The candidate has given the formula to be used in the calculation. You should always do this — it helps the examiner to check the work. The calculation for fixed costs is incorrect; it should have used the overhead absorption rates to arrive at £686 000 (20 000 × 30 + 10 000 × 8.60). The remainder of the answer is accurate and once again is supported by clear workings. Candidate A scores 5 marks.

(c)

Margin of safety = sales – b/e
                 = 12 000 – 8579
                 = 3421

$\dfrac{3421}{12\,000}$ ✓* ✓ = 28.51% ✓*

✎ This answer scores 3 marks. This is a good, accurate response using the candidate's own figures.

(d) A 10% pay rise is an extra £2.20 on top of the £128.35 already calculated.

so this =	£130.55 ✓	
Mark up	26.11 ✓	
	156.66 ✓	
Less VC	66.20 ✓	(64.00 + 2.20)
New contribution	90.46	

New B/E $\dfrac{772\ 200}{90.46}$ ✓* = 8537 units ✓*
           ✓

$\dfrac{42}{8579}$ = 0.005% ✓*

> This is another well thought out and worked answer and it scores maximum marks. The candidate has used the incorrect fixed costs from part (b) so is awarded an own figure mark. Again good workings are shown.

(e) Break-even analysis is a useful tool for business managers. It allows them to see the point at which the business makes neither a profit nor a loss. ✓ If sales fall below this point, they know that the business is in trouble; above this point they know that they will be making profits. ✓ They can calculate the margin of safety from this analysis by taking the break-even point from the budgeted level of sales. The margin of safety tells them by how much they can let sales slide ✓ before they are in the problem area. So B/E analysis is very useful.

But managers must always remember that there are limitations. ✓ For example, assumptions are made that:
- all data behave in a linear manner
- the only thing that affects costs and revenues is the level of sales ✓
- all production is sold
- there are no opening or closing inventories
- the cost mix remains consistent

Break-even charts are easy to understand but they can be inaccurate. On the whole they are very useful provided managers remember the limitations, but I think that the benefits outweigh the limitations. ✓

> A few good points have been made but the candidate seems to be rushing to finish the discussion. The answer might have benefited from a plan. This generally helps candidates to gather their thoughts. As far as the second part of the answer is concerned, the candidate shows some knowledge but it is not clear whether there is understanding and certainly there is no attempt to apply the limitations; some of the limitations discussed are applicable to break-even charts. There is a limited attempt at a judgement, but again there is little attempt to justify the conclusion.

> **There are large gaps in the answers to parts (b) and (e) but otherwise there are some very good points. The answers are well laid out and supported by detailed workings. A total of 28 marks out of 35 are scored, which is a grade-A answer.**

■ ■ ■

Answer to question 5: candidate B

(a)

Mats	42.00	✓
Wages	22.00	✓
O/h A	50.00	
B	7.16	
	121.16	
Profit	24.23	✓*
SP	145.39	✓*

> This answer scores 4 marks. The candidate should have used a heading. The overhead charges are incorrect. The examiner cannot determine where the errors have occurred since the figures are not supported by workings. The other amounts have been calculated accurately.

(b) B/E $\frac{57.16}{81.39}$ = 0.7 units so 1 ✓ to the nearest whole number above.
 ✓ ✓ ✓

> This clearly is an incorrect solution, which scores 4 marks. When candidates see a ridiculously low break-even point the error usually lies in the calculation of total fixed costs. The candidate has used his or her own figure for fixed costs per unit rather than total fixed costs. The formula to be used has not been given. Always show a formula.

(c) $\frac{11\ 999}{12\ 000}$ ✓* ✓ = 99.99% ✓*

> This answer scores 3 marks. There is no heading. All calculations and statements should have headings; there may well be a quality of presentation mark available for this. Using the candidate's own figures from part (b), the answer, although unlikely, is correct. Again, such results should ring alarm bells and alert the candidate to the fact that an error has occurred earlier.

(d) 22.00 = 2.20
 42 + 22 + 2.20 = 66.20 Contribution 145.39 – 66.20 ✓ 79.19
 Fixed costs 12 000 × 57.16 = 685 920

 B/E $\frac{685\ 920}{79.19}$ = 8662 units ✓*
 ✓

 $\frac{8662}{1}$ = 8662% ✓*

> This is a much better attempt than in part (b) and 4 marks are scored. However, the candidate has not incorporated the extra wages into the calculation to arrive at the new selling price. Fixed costs are incorrect again but contribution per unit used the correct principle so the new break-even is a more sensible result. The increase is calculated correctly using the candidate's own figures.

(e) They are good to do if you can draw them accurately. You should make sure that the scale used is as big as possible and you should use a sharp pencil because if the lines are too thick it is difficult to get accurate readings. They are much easier to understand than a jumble of figures; especially if people are not accountants, they can be misinterpreted. As well as drawing a graph there are two formula methods. These are probably more accurate than a graph but you can check your graph by doing one of the formulas.

> The candidate has limited the answer to a superficial critique of break-even charts. Rather than discussing the benefits and limitations of the data used, he has focused on the physical production of the charts. There is no attempt at a judgement. This is a poor effort from an A2 candidate. There is nothing to warrant any marks.

> **Overall, this is a borderline pass grade scoring 15 marks. With a little more focus and more workings, this script could have improved the grade received.**

Question 6

Activity based costing (ABC)

Ildiko plc manufactures a variety of products in three departments. The managers have produced an overhead analysis statement for March.

They have used a variety of bases to apportion overhead expenses to the three departments. For example:

- **Rent and rates have been apportioned using the percentage of floor area occupied by each department.**

- **Supervisory wages have been apportioned using the numbers of workers in each department.**

- **Depreciation of machinery has been apportioned by using the cost of the machinery used in each department.**

The finance director has recently heard of activity based costing (ABC). She asks you to prepare a memorandum for presentation to the board of directors.

REQUIRED

Prepare a memorandum for presentation to the board of directors of Ildiko plc explaining activity based costing and discussing the implications of its implementation.

(18 marks)

plus 2 marks for quality of written communication

■ ■ ■

Answer to question 6: candidate A

Plan: heading abc adv-accy in cstg more eff truer contr not all v costly driver pool

> The candidate has used a plan. This enables the content of the memorandum to be organised in a logical manner and to avoid repetition of any points. It does not have to make sense to anyone other than the candidate, so abbreviations or any other form of shorthand may be used.

To: The board of directors

From: Thomas Parkes

Date: 26 February 2010

Subject: Explanation of the term 'activity based costing'. The advantages and disadvantages of using it in your company.

MEMORANDUM

> The candidate has used a clear memorandum format and it scores the mark allocated. The heading is explicit and unambiguous.

Activity based costing is a type of costing that apportions overhead costs to products according to how much of the overhead has actually been used in the manufacture of the product. ✓ At present the overheads are being apportioned to a department according to the area taken up by each department or by the cost of machinery or by the numbers of people working in the department. These bases do not take into account that some products take up little space or have little machining or have little time in the hands of a worker. ✓

> The opening paragraph shows that the candidate understands the approach that ABC uses; he or she also gives a couple of examples to develop the argument.

There are three cost pools mentioned in the question: rent and rates, supervisory wages and depreciation. ✓ It would be much more accurate if the company allocated these costs by identifying cost drivers in each case. ✓ The rent and rates could be allocated according to the time that each product takes to go through the department. ✓ The supervisory wages could be allocated according to the time supervisors have to spend making sure that each worker produces a perfect product. ✓ The depreciation could be allocated according to the amount of time each product spends in the machine. ✓

> The candidate explains what is meant by the terms 'cost pool' and 'cost driver' and again develops the points with the use of examples.

As you can see this is a much more accurate way of allocating costs to a product (rather than apportioning them on some arbitrary basis). ✓ This means that the whole costing process is much more efficient and gives a better picture of the true cost of the product. ✓ If managers have a good idea of the true cost of manufacturing a product, they can easily see where costs are accumulating ✓ and start to implement policies that can control the costs. ✓ This will cut down on waste. ✓

> The candidate outlines some advantages of using ABC and develops them clearly.

The downside of going over to ABC is that it can be costly to put in place. ✓ For example, someone would have to time exactly how long each product spends in a particular machine and how much time each supervisor spends with each worker as he or she works on a product. ✓ Some people have said that the costs involved are too high and question whether all the hassle is worth it.

There is also the problem that not all costs can be easily attributed to a product. ✓ For example, when the accounts department is preparing the end-of-year financial statements, where will the cost be allocated? How will the CEO's salary be allocated?

> The discussion continues as the candidate outlines the problems that could be encountered if a system of ABC was introduced.

Conclusion

I think that ABC is a very good system and that you should implement it in your company ✓ even though there may be some overheads that cannot be allocated and it might be expensive to put in place. It will probably save you money because you will be able to see where costs are being wasted and you can then put policies in place that will cut out this waste. ✓

🖉 A discussion always needs a conclusion. The candidate provides one and makes sure that the examiner recognises this by using a sub-heading.

🖉 **This is a grade-A answer. The candidate has given a balanced memorandum and scores 15 marks for the 'body' of the answer, 2 for the quality of written communication including the memorandum format and 2 for the conclusion.**

■ ■ ■

Answer to question 6: candidate B

ABC stands for activity based costing. This is an alternative system to absorption and marginal costing. It is a lot more expensive to run than the other two. ✓ It reflects the resources actually used in the making of the product. ✓

The costs of running a resource are gathered together in a cost pool. ✓ They are then split between the various products being made by using cost drivers. ✓ Imagine a toy maker. If it takes 1 hour to make a toy train and 3 hours to make a fort, the cost driver would allocate three times as much rent and rates to the fort than he does to the train. ✓ With depreciation, if the cost driver uses a power tool there would be three times as much depreciation allocated to the fort as to the train.

🖉 This is a reasonable opening paragraph, which indicates that the candidate understands the basics of activity based costing. However, a 'quality' mark could have been earned by using a memorandum heading. The candidate gives the impression that he or she believes a cost driver to be a person.

This has got to be a lot more accurate ✓ than just allocating all the rent and rates to the section where trains and forts are made and splitting it between the two in an arbitrary way. ABC can be used to control costs. ✓ You can look at the pool and if it is too big then you can find ways of reducing it by finding alternative suppliers of that resource.

🖉 Two advantages are outlined here. The two points could have been developed, giving the examiner more evidence of understanding and application.

Direct costs are easy to allocate but other costs are difficult ✓ and ABC will help you to do this. Activity is the important word in the title — the more activity involved, the higher most costs will be that should go onto the costing sheet for each product. ✓ So the cost driver will allocate his cost pools to the products made according to the activity undergone in making the product.

The candidate recognises that overheads are difficult to allocate, hence the need for some way to apportion them. He or she also understands that the main thrust of activity based costing is the amount of activity involved in the production process for each product. It is again evident that the candidate believes that a cost driver is a person.

This answer would have benefited from a plan, to give a more logical approach to the whole answer. The answer lacks the conclusion that is necessary when discussing a topic.

The candidate scores 9 marks, which is sufficient to gain a marginal pass grade.

Standard costing

Boris Krupp Ltd manufactures plastic garden furniture. The furniture is manufactured from sheets of plastic purchased ready for use.

The following statement has been produced to show the contribution made by the garden furniture to overall company results for the year ended 31 December 2009.

Contribution statement (garden furniture) for the year ended 31 December 2009

	£	£
Sales		972 000
Variable costs		
Raw materials	274 950	
Direct labour	128 800	403 750
Contribution		568 250

There were no opening or closing stocks of furniture.

Additional information

(1) The budget and standard cost details prepared prior to 1 January 2009 were:

(i) budgeted sales of furniture was 27 000 sets at £42.00 per set

(ii) each set of furniture should use 2.5 kg of plastic at £4.50 per kilogram

(iii) each set of furniture should take 30 minutes of direct labour time

(iv) direct labour was to be paid at £9 per hour

(2) When the actual results for the year ended 31 December 2009 were compiled, it emerged that:

(i) 24 000 sets of furniture were sold

(ii) 58 500 kg of plastic were used

(iii) 14 000 hours of direct labour time were used

REQUIRED

(a) Calculate:

(i) the sales volume variance

(ii) the sales price variance

(iii) the total sales variance

(iv) the raw materials usage variance

(v)   the raw materials price variance

(vi) the total materials variance

(vii) the direct labour efficiency variance

(viii) the direct labour rate variance

(ix) the total direct labour variance   (18 marks)

(b) **Prepare a statement showing the budgeted contribution and reconciling this to the actual contribution.**   (12 marks)

(c) **Outline a possible interrelationship between the following variances calculated in (a):**

    (i)   **the raw materials usage variance and the raw materials price variance**   (3 marks)

    (ii) **the raw materials price variance and the direct labour rate variance**   (3 marks)

(d) **Discuss why a favourable total labour variance may not be desirable.**   (7 marks)

plus 2 marks for quality of written communication

Answer to question 7: candidate A

(a) Sales

Sq × Sp   27 000 × 42   = 1 134 000

                                 126 000   adv volume variance ✓ ✓

Aq × Sp   24 000 × 42   = 1 008 000

                                  36 000   adv price variance ✓ ✓

Aq × Ap   24 000 × 40.50 =   972 000 _____

                              162 000   adv total sales variance ✓ ✓

Materials

Sq × Sp   67 500 × 4.50   = 303 750

                              40 500   fav usage variance

Aq × Sp   58 500 × 4.50   = 263 250

                             11 700   adverse price variance ✓ ✓

Aq × Ap   58 500 × 4.70   = 274 950 _____

                            28 800   fav total materials variance ✓ ✓*

Labour

Sq × Sp 13 500 × 9   = 121 500

4 500   ad efficiency variance

Aq × Sp 14 000 × 9   = 126 000

2 800   ad rate variance ✓ ✓

Aq × Ap 14 000 × 9.20 = 128 800

7 300   ad total labour variance ✓ ✓*

📝 This is a well laid out answer that scores 14 marks. It uses 'the grid', in the main, accurately. The only error is that the candidate has failed to adjust (flex) the budget to take into account the lower sales (hence production) levels in the standard quantities of materials and labour. Only $\frac{8}{9}$ of standard production was completed, so standard quantities of materials and labour should have been flexed to reflect this.

(b)   ***Reconciliation of budgeted contribution to actual contribution***

Budgeted sales   1 134 000 ✓ 27000 × 42
Sales variances   – volume   (126 000) ✓
          – price   (36 000) ✓
Materials variance – usage   40 500 ✓*
          – price   (11 700) ✓
Labour variances   – efficiency (4 500) ✓*
          – rate   (2 800) ✓
Actual contribution   964 700

📝 This is another well laid out and labelled answer, which scores 7 marks. The candidate should have shown actual sales (£972 000) as a sub-total. He or she should also have deducted £378 000 (24 000 × 11.25 + 4.50), the standard cost of actual sales, to give the budgeted contribution. Nevertheless, overall this is a good attempt using the candidate's own figures from part (a).

(c) (i) The raw materials usage variance is favourable to the business probably because the materials are better quality ✓ than those in the budget. ✓ This shows up as an adverse price variance ✓ because better quality materials usually cost more than poorer quality materials. ✓

📝 The maximum 3 marks are scored.

(ii) The material price variance is adverse because more expensive materials have been bought, ✓ so this means that they are probably better quality than the managers budgeted for. ✓ Because of the more expensive, better materials, the managers may have hired more experienced staff that cost more in wages ✓ or they may have paid existing staff 20p more per hour to encourage them to take more care with the materials. ✓

This answer scores the maximum 3 marks. The candidate gives two good examples of interrelationships. He has identified the factors and then gone on to develop the ideas in a detailed way.

(d) A favourable labour variance is made up of an efficiency variance and a wage rate variance.

If the labour variance is favorable, this could indicate that fewer labour hours have been used. ✓ Has the work been rushed, ✓ giving a poor quality product to go to customers? ✓ This might lose future sales. ✓ If the labour rate is favourable, it means that we have paid our workforce cheaper so they are likely to be more unskilled than we budgeted for. ✓ The workers could waste more materials ✓ and so once again a poor quality product might be the result ✓ and once again we may loose customers because of the poor quality. ✓ These customers might spread the 'bad news' of a poor quality product and so deter future customers. ✓ So all in all, although we are saving money, there might be repercussions and it might not be such a good thing.

This is a detailed response that scores the maximum 7 marks. It explains why a favourable labour variance might not be such a good thing. There are a few grammatical and spelling errors but this does not detract from the content. It does, however, mean that only 1 of the 2 marks for quality of written communication can be awarded.

The candidate scores 35 marks out of a possible 45, which is a comfortable grade A, for a well balanced answer that contains only a few errors.

■ ■ ■

Answer to question 7: candidate B

(a) P = (Stand – Act) × Act qy
Q = (Stand quan – Act quan) × S pr

Sales (42 – 40.5) × 24 000   =   36 000 fav price ✓
(27 000 × 24 000) × 42 = 126 000 fav vol ✓
162 000 tot fav ✓ ✓*

Mat (4.50 – 4.70) × 58 500 =   11 700 fav price ✓
54 000 (4.50 – 4.70)   =   10 800 adv quantity
900 fav tot ✓ ✓

Lab (9 – 9.20) × 54 000   =   10 800 fav price
(54 000 – 14 000) × 9 = 360 000 fav quantity
370 000 fav total ✓ ✓*

This answer scores 9 marks. Although the calculations for the two sales variances are arithmetically correct, the 'direction' is incorrect; both should be adverse variances. The same error is made in the calculation of the material price variance. The candidate has not flexed the direct standard costs and has not calculated correctly the standard number of labour hours used.

(b)

Sales	1 134 000 ✓
Variance	162 000 ✓ ✓*
Budgeted contribution	1 296 000
Materials variance	(900)
Labour variance	(370 800)
Actual contribution	924 300

✏ This answer scores 3 marks. The budgeted contribution is miscalculated, although the adjustment to budgeted sales is made correctly using the candidate's own figures. The directions of the direct materials variances are in the wrong direction. The actual contribution calculated does not agree with the actual contribution given in the stem of the question.

(c) The raw materials usage variance is adverse, meaning that they paid more for the materials than they budgeted for. This will cause profit to go down as it increases their expenses. These materials will be good if they are paying more for them but they will most probably have to put prices up. The favourable price variance means that they have paid a good price for the materials. This could be due to them shopping around and paying a good supplier a decent price.

✏ This is a confused response. The usage variance is confused with the price variance. The candidate has misunderstood the cause of the 'direction' of the price variance.

(d) A favourable labour variance means that workers are working well for the company and that they are producing goods that will sell well. The company could use its good workers as a marketing tool by emphasising that workers are favourable to the company and are happy in their work. This will create a good image for the company, which will probably increase profits and so the company can give the workers a pay rise, making them more favourable in the future and creating more good marketing publicity, which could lead to more customers

✏ The candidate is very confused. He or she has not focused on the causes of a favourable labour variance and how this might have arisen through the labour rate and labour efficiency. The only saving grace is the 1 quality mark awarded.

✏ **This is a poor attempt by an A2 candidate. Greater care in the calculations required in parts (a) and (b) might have lifted the total mark over the pass/fail threshold. In addition, a focus on the likely causes of variances could have given the candidate more marks. As it is, a total of 13 marks were scored out of a possible 45, which is insufficient to gain a pass grade.**

Question 8

Capital investment appraisal

The managers of Sharris plc need to replace an obsolete machine. They are considering choosing from three alternative machines as the replacement:

The **XY78** is manufactured in Japan.

The **EUC5** is manufactured in the EU.

The **USD9** is manufactured in the USA.

The following information is available for the machines:

	XY78	EUC5	USD9
Cost of machine	£110 000	£80 000	£90 000

The following additional information is available for the FUC5 and the USD9:

	EUC5		USD9	
	Net cash flows	NPV	Net cash flows	NPV
	£	£	£	£
Year 0	(80 000)	(80 000)	(90 000)	(90 000)
Year 1	60 000	54 540	22 000	19 998
Year 2	60 000	49 560	22 000	18 172
Year 3	60 000	45 060	23 000	17 273
Year 4	60 000	40 980	23 000	15 709
	NPV	110 140	NPV	(18 848)

The information for machine **XY78** has still to be calculated.

Cash flows	Revenues	Operating expenses
	£	£
Year 1	70 000	15 000
Year 2	74 000	16 000
Year 3	79 000	18 000
Year 4	83 000	20 000

In addition to the above operating expenses, the **XY78** will require a major overhaul in years 2 and 4. Both overhauls will costs £3500.

The current cost of capital for Sharris plc is 10%.

Assume that all cash flows arise evenly throughout the year when calculating payback periods and that they arise at the end of the relevant year when calculating net present value.

An extract from the present value table for £1 at 10% is shown:

Year	10%
1	0.909
2	0.826
3	0.751
4	0.683

REQUIRED

(a) Calculate the net present value for machine **XY78**.   (12 marks)

(b) Calculate for each machine:

   (i)   the payback period   (5 marks)

   (ii) the discounted payback period   (5 marks)

(c) Advise Sharris plc which machine should be purchased.   (8 marks)

■ ■ ■

Answer to question 8: candidate A

(a)   *The net present value of machine XY78*

Year	Cash flows	Discount factor	NPV
	£		£
0	(110 000) ✓	1	(110 000) ✓
1	55 000 ✓	0.909	49 995 ✓
2	54 500 ✓	0.826	45 017 ✓
3	61 000 ✓	0.751	45 811 ✓
4	59 500 ✓	0.683	40 638.50 ✓
		Net present value ✓	71 461.50 ✓

🖉 This is a perfect answer, scoring the full 12 marks. There is a good heading and the layout is clear and concise. The calculations are accurate and the final total is clearly labelled.

(b) (i) XY78 Payback 2 years and 500/61 000   = 2.008 years ✓ ✓
         EUC5 Payback 1 year and 20 000/60 000 = 1.33 years ✓ ✓
         USD9 Payback 4 years exactly ✓

🖉 The candidate gives another clear, concise answer here, scoring all 5 marks. The examiner is in no doubt what the candidate has calculated and what each payback period is. The calculations of the fractions of the year are also clear.

(ii) XY78 Discounted payback 2 years and 14 988/45 811 = 2.33 years ✓ ✓
      EUC5 Discounted payback 1 year and 25 460/49 560 = 1.51 years ✓ ✓
      USD9 Discounted payback 4 years less 18 848/90 000 = 3.79 years

🖉 Four marks are scored. The first two answers are accurate but the candidate is confused by the negative net present value, indicating that the machine USD9 will not payback in the 4 years.

(c) To: The managers of Sharris plc

From: Jill Brown

Date xx/xx/xx

Subject: Advice on the purchase of a new machine

You should purchase the machine manufactured in the EU — machine EUC5 ✓ because it has the fastest payback period ✓ by about 7 months. ✓ It also has a superior net present value, ✓ indicating that it has the best cash flows even when discounted at 10% per annum. ✓ (This percentage is the cost of capital.) A criticism of the payback system of capital investment appraisal is that it does not take into account the time value of money, so the discounted payback method gets round this. ✓ Using this method, it pays back in 18 months, ✓ still better than the other two machines. It also has a lower initial outlay, ✓ so if you buy this machine you may have surplus funds available to use elsewhere in your business. ✓ Another advantage is that the machine is manufactured nearer to the UK and so spares may be obtained more easily ✓ than having to ship them half way across the world or the Atlantic. ✓ If workers need to be trained to use the machine, the manufacturer is close so its experts can get to the UK much easier or your workers could go there more easily.

For all these reasons I would advise you to purchase the EUC5. I can't see many disadvantages.

  The maximum **8 marks** are scored. The candidate has given a full, comprehensive answer outlining which machine should be chosen. He or she has developed each point in turn. It is pleasing to note that the candidate has widened the answer to include some non-financial factors, i.e. the proximity of the supplier and possible training needs.

  One criticism: the question did not ask for a memorandum or brief report so the heading is superfluous and took up valuable time.

  Overall, this candidate scores **29 out of a possible 30 marks, achieving a comfortable grade A.**

■ ■ ■

Answer to question 8: candidate B

(a)

55 000 ✓	49 995 ✓
58 000	47 980
61 000 ✓	45 811 ✓
63 000	43 029 ✓*
237 000	186 815

The candidate seems to understand the basic principles, and has scored 5 marks, but the approach is careless. The answer lacks a heading, indications of the years involved and what each column contains. The candidate has not taken into account the two overhauls costing £3500 in years 2 and 4 and has transposed figures in year 2 — the amount should be £47 908. The cash flows should total £76 815 using the candidate's own figures; he or she has not taken the initial cost from the net cash flows.

(b)(i) 1.95 years ✓ ✓*
1.33 years ✓ ✓
4 years ✓

The payback period has not caused the candidate any problems; he or she scores maximum marks.

(ii) 2.28 years ✓   110 000 – 97 975 = 12 025/43 029
1.51 years ✓ ✓   80 000 – 54 500 = 25 460/49 560
?

The candidate knows how to calculate the discounted payback but in the first calculation he or she has used the discounted cash flows for year 4 rather than year 3, another careless mistake. The candidate was also possibly confused by the negative discounted cash flow.

(c) Go for machine XY78. ✓ The payback for the second machine is faster both times ✓ but it is not much faster — 6 months and 7 months. However, the net present value is vastly superior for the first machine ✓ — over £75 000 more; this is a lot. Furthermore, Japanese machines will be good — their televisions and computers are the best.

This answer scores 3 marks. The candidate gives advice and the reasoning is sound. However, the calculation of 6 months and 7 months is inaccurate (7.44 months and 9.24 months) and there is a failure to widen the advice to discuss some of the factors that candidate A introduced.

Overall the candidate scores a comfortable pass grade with 16 out of a possible 30 marks but could have improved on this by being more focused and less careless.

Budgets and budgetary control

Ragesh Shah has prepared the following cash budgets for the 5 months ending 31 May 2010.

	January £	February £	March £	April £	May £
Receipts					
Sales – cash	14 000	25 200	28 000	33 600	32 200
Cash credit customers	17 400	6 000	10 800	12 000	14 400
	31 400	31 200	38 800	45 600	46 600
Payments					
Cash purchases	10 500	9 000	9 500	12 500	12 000
Cash to credit customers	11 500	14 000	10 500	9 000	9 500
Deposit on purchase of vehicle		10 000			
Balance of vehicles purchase price					20 000
Wages	8 000	7 000	7 000	9 000	7 000
General expenses	3 100	3 000	2 800	4 700	4 000
	33 100	43 000	29 800	35 200	52 500
Balance b/fwd	4 460	2 760	(9 040)	40	10 440
Receipts	31 400	31 200	38 800	45 600	46 600
	35 860	33 960	29 760	45 640	57 040
Payments	33 100	43 000	29 800	35 200	52 500
Balance c/fwd	2 760	(9 040)	40	10 440	4 540

The cash budget was prepared using the following information.

It was expected that:

- **70% sales will be for cash — credit customers were expected to pay in the month following the sales.**

- **50% of purchases will be for cash — credit suppliers were expected to be paid 2 months after the purchases were made.**

- **A vehicle will be purchased in February — a deposit of £10 000 to be paid on purchase and the balance to be paid in May.**

- **Wages will be paid 1 month after being incurred.**

- **General expenses will be paid when incurred.**

Additional information

(1) Non-current assets at 1 January 2010 will be valued at cost £150 000.

(2) All non-current assets are depreciated at 10% per annum on cost.

(3) Inventory at 1 January 2010 is expected to be £18 000 and at 31 March 2010 it is expected to be £19 000.

REQUIRED

(a) Prepare a trade receivables' (debtors') budget for the 3 months ending 31 March 2010. (6 marks)

(b) Prepare a trade payables' (creditors') budget for the 3 months ending 31 March 2010. (12 marks)

(c) Prepare a forecast income statement for the 3 months ending 31 March 2010. (18 marks)

(d) Evaluate the benefits that a business might hope to gain through the preparation of budgets. (14 marks)

■ ■ ■

Answer to question 9: candidate A

(a)

Receivables budget

	Jan	Feb	Mar
Balance b/d	17 400 ✓	6 000 ✓	10 800 ✓
Credit sales	6 000	10 800	12 000
	23 400	16 800	22 800
Receipts	17 400	6 000	10 800
Balance c/d	6 000 ✓	10 800 ✓	12 000 ✓

✎ This is a well-prepared budget that scores the maximum 6 marks.

(b)

Payables budget

	Jan	Feb	Mar
Balance b/d	25 500 ✓	24 500 ✓	19 500 ✓
Purchases	10 500 ✓	9 000 ✓	9 500 ✓
	36 000	33 500	29 000
Payments	11 500 ✓	14 000 ✓	10 500 ✓
Balance c/d	24 500 ✓	19 500 ✓	18 500 ✓

✎ The candidate gives another neat and well laid-out budget. Neatness always helps when casting monthly totals. The maximum 12 marks are scored.

(c) **R. Shah forecast income statement for the year ended 31 March 2010**

	£	£
Sales		96 000 ✓ ✓ ✓
Inventory	18 000 ✓	
Purchases	58 000 ✓ ✓ ✓	
Inventory	19 000 ✓	57 000
Gross profit		39 000 ✓
Wages	23 000 ✓ ✓ ✓	
General expenses	8 900 ✓	
Depreciation	15 000 ✓	46 900
Profit for year		7 900

Workings: Sales 20 000 + 36 000 + 40 000
Purch. 21 000 + 18 000 + 19 000
Dep. 150 000 × 10%

This is a sound answer, scoring 14 marks. The layout is good and the candidate has calculated all the figures accurately with the exception of depreciation. Depreciation has been calculated on existing non-current assets. The total cost of all non-current assets should have been used, i.e. £180 000. The depreciation should also have been calculated for only the 3 months, giving £4500. It is good to see so many workings supporting the main body of the income statement. The answer was marred by a couple of basic errors. The heading should have indicated that the income statement was for the 3 months ending 31 March 2010 and the profit is in fact a loss of £7900 (own figure).

(d) Plan: Yes PCCC cash balances No — demot — perf rivalry

It is good to see that the candidate has used a plan to determine what to write. A plan also means that once a point has been made it can be 'ticked off' — this avoids candidates making the same point two or three times. Apart from the last sentence the candidate has stuck to the plan.

Businesses should prepare budgets. ✓ They help the owners of a business to plan, control, coordinate and communicate. ✓ By doing a cash budget it helps the managers to see if they need to go overdrawn at the bank, e.g. February, ✓ or if they have plenty spare. ✓ If they have to go overdrawn, they can arrange this with the bank well ahead of time ✓ and this will probably be cheaper than just going overdrawn without telling the bank beforehand. ✓ They seem to have a lot of spare cash in April and May; this could be put in a high interest account to earn extra cash. ✓ The trouble with budgets is that the forecasts used to prepare them might be inaccurate because things can occur between preparing the budget and its actual happening. ✓ If budgets are easily achieved, members of the department can just coast along. ✓ If the budget can't be achieved, the workers and managers in that section might become demotivated ✓ and it could affect their performance. ✓ Budgets can make departments rivals for resources. ✓

I think that all businesses should prepare budgets ✓ because they cause planning, controlling, coordinating and communicating.

🖉 This answer scores 13 marks. The question was directed at budgets in general; the candidate has concentrated on cash budgets but has managed to bring out the major advantages and disadvantages of budgets in general using cash budgets as the focus. The points made are developed well and the candidate has used the question to give an example, showing good application.

🖉 **Overall, this is a comfortable grade A scoring 45 out of a possible 50 marks.**

■ ■ ■

Answer to question 9: candidate B

(a)

	Jan	**Feb**	**Mar**
Balance	31 400	45 400 ✓ *	70 600 ✓*
Sales	31 400	31 200	38 800
	62 800	76 600	109 400
Cash	17 400	6 000	10 800
Balance	45 400	70 600	98 600

🖉 Only the process is rewarded for 2 marks. The candidate knows how to lay out the budget but clearly does not know where the sales figures and opening balance come from. The candidate has used cash sales and the previous months' credit sales rather than just the credit sales made in each month.

(b)

	Jan	**Feb**	**Mar**
Balance	22 000	32 500 ✓	41 500 ✓
Purchases	22 000	33 000	20 000
	44 000	65 500	61 500
Cash	11 500 ✓	24 000	10 500 ✓
	32 500 ✓*	41 500 ✓*	51 000 ✓*

🖉 This answer scores 7 marks. Once again the layout is good. Cash purchases and credit purchases are combined. The February cash includes a non-trade payable (the deposit on the vehicle). The balances are calculated accurately using the candidate's own figures and they are carried forward accurately.

(c)

Income statement for the year ended 31 Mar 09

	£	£	
Sales		101 400	31 400 + 31 200 + 38 800
Inventory	18 000 ✓		
Purchases	65 000		22 000 + 23 000 + 20 000
	83 000		
Inventory	19 000 ✓	64 000	
GP		37 800	
Less expenses			
Wages	22 000 ✓ ✓		8000 + 7000 + 7000
General exps	8 900 ✓		
Depn	14 000	44 900	140 000 × 10%
Loss for year		(7 100) ✓ᵗʰ	

This income statement is laid out well, although the use of the word 'year' rather than 'the 3 months ending' and the use of '09' rather than 2010 mean that the heading mark cannot be awarded. The abbreviation 'GP' means that the own figure mark for gross profit is lost. Purchases and sales are calculated incorrectly but the good practice of showing workings is to be applauded. The workings achieve 2 part marks for the incorrect wages total. If the candidate had used a calculator and used £22 000 without showing workings, both marks would have been lost. The same comment applies to the calculation for depreciation. The candidate has scored 1 mark for the own loss figure, which is correctly labelled. This answer scores 6 marks.

(d) Budgets are used for planning, coordinating, communicating, decision making and controlling. ✓ All of these are good things. ✓

The candidate has clearly learned part of a text on budgeting and has listed uses and the types of budget that a business might prepare. However, there is no attempt to develop these points. There is an unsupported evaluation in the second sentence.

You should use them for sales budgets, production budgets, purchases budgets, trade receivables budgets, trade payables budgets, cash budgets and master budgets. ✓ Master budgets are really just a budgeted income account. If a company does not do budgets, each department will run out of money and the company will probably have to get a loan from the bank. So they might have to pay a lot of interest. If interest rates are high, it cannot afford this and the company will go bust. ✓

This answer scores 4 marks. The candidate hints at the consequences of inadequate control being exercised through budgets by indicating that the business might go into liquidation through mismanagement of resources.

Overall, there is not quite enough depth in any section to score a pass grade so the candidate marginally fails. The candidate scores 19 out of a possible 50. With more focus and depth of understanding, this mark could easily have been lifted above the E-grade boundary.

Social accounting

Karpluk Ltd manufactures paper for the printing industry. The present process uses old machinery that is currently blamed for polluting the local river in the cooling process and polluting the air around the factory. The company is currently making annual losses. The directors are considering the purchase of a new automated production line manufactured in Sweden. The manufacturers claim zero pollution using their equipment.

The directors' forecast income statements based on using the new production line show that the business should achieve significant profits in the years following installation.

Installation of the new production line would mean the loss of many jobs at Karpluk Ltd.

REQUIRED

Prepare a short report advising the directors of Karpluk Ltd whether or not the old equipment should be replaced with the new production line. Give all your arguments for and against your decision.

(20 marks)

plus 2 marks for quality of written communication

■ ■ ■

Answer to question 10: candidate A

Plan: losses — survival need pr;
        pollution — not good — affect pr
        workers — families/local/national

🗲 It is always good to see a plan.

To: The directors

From: Jane Brown

Date (as per examination)

Subject: Advise on replacing existing equipment with new Swedish production line.

I am going to cover three aspects in my report:
- losses
- pollution
- staff

(1) The company is currently making annual losses and therefore action must be taken. If this problem is not addressed then the company will not survive. ✓ Profits are necessary for long-term survival. ✓ The purchase of the new equipment from Sweden might solve this problem. You have prepared some forecast income statements for the future. How reliable are these projections? ✓ How likely is it that the profits shown can be trusted? Future sales have been estimated but what if new businesses come into the industry? ✓ Sales could go down. ✓ There could be inflation in the future, which would put up all your costs. ✓ Before purchasing the new equipment, the causes of the annual losses should be investigated fully to make sure that buying the new machinery really would solve the problem. ✓

> ✎ Although rather rambling in places, this is a well thought out paragraph, scoring 6 marks. The candidate outlines the necessity of being profitable for long-term survival. There is a good section on the reliability of projected income statements and a mark is awarded for the development using examples. The candidate also queries the action to be taken prior to any purchase.

(2) Pollution is a great problem these days. At the moment the company is a polluter. Buying the new machinery will cut down on this; in fact the Swedish people reckon there is no impact on the environment. This must be good. ✓ At the moment the pollution will be getting the company bad publicity, which may be affecting sales ✓ and this may be the reason for the company making losses. ✓

The company might be affected by pressure group action, which might result in more bad publicity. ✓

New, cleaner machinery will restore the credibility of the company and will result in more customers.

> ✎ Much of the first few lines merely repeats information given in the question. The candidate links levels of sales with pollution, which may well be true. The candidate appears to have forgotten the final product (paper for the printing industry). Four marks are scored here.

(3) If the company installs the new production line, a great many jobs will be lost. This will affect the families of workers by reducing their income ✓ and this will have a multiplier effect ✓ because the families will not be able to spend as much in local shops, so they could be affected too. ✓ It means that the government will be affected because it will not get the income taxes and it will have to pay out a lot more in benefits. ✓ There could be a loss of morale in the business. ✓ The workers that are left will wonder if their jobs are the next to go. ✓ If morale goes down, the quality of the product might suffer and the new profits might not be as big as first thought. ✓

> ✎ Six marks are awarded for this part. This is another good section where points have been identified and then developed. The candidate scores both quality of written communication marks.

This answer is marred by the lack of advice required in the question. Despite this lapse, the candidate scores 18 marks, which is sufficient for a comfortable grade A.

■ ■ ■

Answer to question 10: candidate B

I think that the directors should install the new machinery ✓ because the environment is very important. The pollution causes global warming and unless we do something about it, it may be too late. Our children and children's children will not thank us for being so uncaring. I know that a lot of workers will lose their jobs but this number will be low compared to the many millions that will be affected by the pollution. I think that the workers would understand if it was explained to them — perhaps you could hold a meeting to explain the facts to them.

The redundant workers will not be that badly off. They will get a lump sum on redundancy and they can use this to set up in business. In fact if two or three workers band together, they could start up in partnership. This means that they would have to share profits (and losses) and they would have unlimited liability. But it does mean that if they are ill or need a holiday, there will always be someone there to look after the business.

Pollution is a very bad thing and the publicity that surrounds it is bad too. Bad publicity means less sales ✓ — less sales means less profits ✓ and this is probably what has happened already. The question says so. If the directors get this sorted they will start to make profits again, so perhaps the workers won't have to lose their jobs after all.

Yes, you need to install the new machinery and fast, otherwise the company could go bust and then everybody not just a few would be out of work. This would be a great loss to the government having to pay all that money out in benefits. ✓

The candidate refers to polluting being bad but does not develop this point in any way, for instance to give the effects of pollution on the environment in general or on Karpluk Ltd. The answer lacks focus but does recognise the financial consequences that might affect the government. It also gains 1 mark for written presentation.

This superficial answer scores a total of 5 out of a possible 22 marks, which would not be a pass grade at A2.

Student Feedback Form

Philip Allan Updates would welcome your views so that we can publish exactly the right resources for you. If you complete the following form, you will be entered into a **monthly prize draw** to win a Philip Allan Updates book of your choice.

Student Unit Guide name: AQA A2 Accounting Unit 4: Further Aspects of Management Accounting

Your name: Your school:

e-mail address*:

* So that we can contact you if you win the prize draw.

Why did you decide to buy this guide?

☐ Bought for me by school / college
☐ Recommended by teacher / parent / friend
☐ Found online / in a bookshop
☐ Other _____

Have you found this guide helpful for your studies / revision? _____ Yes / No
_____

How have you used this *Student Unit Guide*?
_____
_____

At what point in the course did you use this *Student Unit Guide*?
_____
_____

Is there anything else you would like from this guide?
_____
_____

What sort of online revision tools do you use?
_____
_____

Would you like to be able to buy revision guides as e-books?_____ Yes / No

Please return your completed form to:
Fax: 01869 338293
Post: Marketing Feedback, Philip Allan Updates, FREEPOST, Deddington, Oxfordshire OX14 0BR
Email: marketing@philipallan.co.uk

Internal use only:

☐ Marketing   ☐ Editorial   ☐ Commissioning Competition month _____